COVER: *The cowboys in this picture by Charles Russell are trying to rope a steer. Roping was often the most complicated part of a cowboy's job and required not only great skill with the use of the catch rope or lariat but it demanded expert horsemanship on the part of the cowboy; he had to perform the most involved operations while riding fast.*

FRONT END SHEET: *The Mexican vaqueros in this painting by James Walker are rounding up a thundering herd of wild horses. Once caught, the horses had to be broken and trained.*

TITLE PAGE: *A ranchero (probably the man dressed in white at center) and his men are shown here sizing up a herd of cattle. The man on the white horse is an Indian vaquero.*

CONTENTS PAGE: *This Arizona vaquero, drawn in 1898, is roping a steer; his trusty horse, accustomed to the pulling and plunging of roped cattle, braces himself with his forelegs.*

BACK END SHEET: *These cowboys are rounding up cattle in California's San Fernando Valley. After the great herds of the missions were broken up, the valley became one of California's most profitable areas for the development of large, privately owned cattle ranches.*

OPPOSITE: *The drunken cowboy in this sketch (made in Abilene, Kansas, in 1868) is celebrating the sale of a large herd of cattle that he has helped drive north from Texas.*

COWBOYS AND CATTLE COUNTRY

ILLUSTRATED WITH PAINTINGS, PRINTS, DRAWINGS, AND PHOTOGRAPHS OF THE PERIOD

BY THE EDITORS OF AMERICAN HERITAGE
The Magazine of History

NARRATIVE BY DON WARD

IN CONSULTATION WITH J. C. DYKES
U. S. Department of Agriculture

COWBOYS
AND CATTLE COUNTRY

PUBLISHED BY AMERICAN HERITAGE
PUBLISHING CO., INC.
NEW YORK

BOOK TRADE DISTRIBUTION BY MEREDITH PRESS

INSTITUTIONAL DISTRIBUTION BY HARPER & BROTHERS

Foreword

Hollywood and television have made of the cowboy something he never was—and their version is far from the truth, as this book makes graphically clear. The cowboy's life was adventurous, but it was also dirty, lonely, and often brutally hard. The trail driver was not a particularly glamorous figure after he had followed a herd of spooky Texas longhorns from below San Antonio to Abilene or Dodge in Kansas. The trails quickly became dusty, and in the spring and early summer the creeks and rivers were often bank-full and there were no bridges. Swimming a herd across a flood-swollen stream was dangerous work; so was turning a stampede or facing a band of Indians demanding toll for crossing their lands.

Fortunately, such working cowboys as Charlie Siringo, Andy Adams, Jim Cook, Teddy Blue (E. C. Abbott), and many of the old trail drivers have left us accounts of life on the range and trail. Perhaps even more important in keeping history straight is the rich pictorial record of the cowboys and the cattle empires left by such great western artists and illustrators as Frederic Remington, Charles M. Russell, and Olaf Seltzer. You will see examples of their work in the pages that follow.

Russell went to Montana in 1880 as a lad of sixteen—Remington paid his first visit to Montana in 1881. Remington had previously attended Yale for two years where he played football on teams captained and coached by the immortal Walter Camp. He had also studied art at Yale, but he found that this training was of little help in painting the western scene. Remington did not stay in the East very long after his trip to Montana, and in 1883 he operated a small sheep ranch in Kansas. This was the only time that he could actually call the West his home, but he was to return to it time and time again to hunt, to fish, to visit and sketch, to accompany the soldiers on Indian campaigns as both artist and reporter.

In the meantime, Charlie Russell had become a part of Montana—he worked on several ranches but never became a top hand for the simple reason that he was too busy sketching or modeling in wax the men, animals, and action around him; he lived with the Indians and attended the roundups and rodeos. Like Remington, Russell left well over three thousand originals—drawings, water colors, oils, and bronzes—as his contribution to the history of the West.

Seltzer arrived in the West in 1892 when the open range days were almost gone. For many years he lived in Great Falls, Montana, where he was in the shadow of the fame of Charlie Russell. It is only recently that his great talent has become more widely known.

The cowboy today is no longer the historic "hired man on horseback" who was willing to do anything so long as it could be done from the topside of a horse. Ranching has changed. The cowboy rides and ropes, but now he must also be an expert jeep driver (a jeep is faster and will go most of the places a horse can), mason, electrician, carpenter, and mechanic. The rancher, too, has become more than just a stock raiser. He is concerned with animal nutrition and with soil, water, and grass conservation. His home has all the modern conveniences; his children go to modern schools.

Nevertheless, as in the days of old, there are still plenty of grueling, tiresome chores to do, and the modern cowboy must do them. Haying, fencing, treating wire cuts, building cattle guards, reseeding depleted ranges, digging stock tanks, castrating, branding, loading, and shipping are not jobs for the weak. The pattern was set over a century ago, and here is the story—of excitement and boredom, of danger and loneliness, of a unique way of life.

J. C. DYKES

FIRST EDITION

LIBRARY OF CONGRESS CATALOGUE CARD NUMBER: 61-18251

Contents

The mission of Santa Barbara (above) in California, founded in 1786, had a great herd of cattle before the mission system was broken up in 1833.

The Vaquero

The first American cowboy was an Indian. He could ride all day, seemingly a part of his short-bodied horse, whose ancestors had been bred for stamina and speed by the Moors of North Africa. He wore a kerchief wrapped around his head, and over it a wide-brimmed, low-crowned hat that protected him from sun or torrential tropic rains. His knee-length pants were buttoned on the side and worn over long drawers, folded into low-heeled, buckskin shoes. A long knife was carried in a scabbard fastened inside the garter on his right leg. His rawhide lariat *(la reata)* was dallied, or looped, to the saddle horn, and the bright shawl he wore in rough weather hung from its coils. Great slabs of cowhide, called *armas* dangled from the saddle horn, handy for him to pull over his legs when he rode through

brush and thorns. His main weapon and tool was the rawhide lariat, as much as 110 feet long, with which he could bring down a wild bull or a human foe.

This colorful figure was the vaquero, the mounted herdsman of Mexico and California—an Indian who had been trained by his Spanish masters to tend the increasing numbers of cattle on the mission ranchos. (After conquering Mexico, Hernando Cortés enslaved many of the Indians and branded them on the cheek with the letter "G," for *guerra,* or war. Some of these unfortunate people were sold to Spanish ranchers, so it is an ironic fact that the first cowboy wore a brand before the cattle did.) The animals were the hardy Andalusian "black cattle," the breed that eventually produced both the fierce fighting bulls of Spain and

Mexican rancheros like the elegant Don José Sepulveda (above) took over the California cattle industry after 1833. They ruled absolutely over ranches that included thousands of acres of grazing land.

14

The vaquero above, working in a roundup, is busting,
or throwing, a young bull; his horse is keeping the
rope taut so that the frightened animal cannot
stand up. The vaquero will next tie the bull's legs.

matanza
Monterey

These drawings of processing centers of the California cattle industry were made by William Rich Hutton, a young American draftsman who went to the former Mexican province of California in 1847 with the American army of occupation. The matanza (above) at Monterey, California, was the place where cattle were slaughtered; their hides are shown drying on racks in the background. The men below are shown boiling fat from cattle to get tallow for candles.

the presidio, or fort] standing by with his sword to see that the Indian who flogged them done his duty."

At the missions the padres selected the most promising male converts to be trained as vaqueros. They had to be trustworthy, since they could not be kept under constant supervision and since many of the *Indios* liked to eat horse meat. The padres patiently instructed their dark-skinned recruits in the proper method of mounting and riding, and it must have been amusing to watch one of the good fathers, in his long brown robes, showing the prospective vaquero how to get into the saddle and stay there.

When cattle were slaughtered for food, it was the custom to let the vaqueros ride them down and kill them with lances; other *Indios* skinned the carcasses and wrapped the tallow in the hides. The natives were also allowed to cut up the carcasses and take shares of meat. At the mission ranches a rodeo, or roundup, was held every seven days, and beef was distributed for the coming week. When it was time to obtain hides and tallow for marketing there were large-scale slaughterings, or *matanzas,* and cattle were driven to the *matanza* grounds, roped, dragged to the butchers, and "stuck."

Life on the colonists' ranchos was widely recognized as good. Although the ranchero and his family worked hard, their adobe-brick ranch house was comfortable and roomy, food was plentiful, and the *Californios* lived graciously. "If I must be cast in sick-ness or destitution on the care of a stranger," one American wrote, "let it be in California."

The *Californios* were magnificent riders, and much of their relaxation, as well as their work, depended on the horse. Men and women thought nothing of traveling a day's journey for a fandango or wedding, for example. Vaqueros and their masters occupied what leisure time they had with games of skill that derived from their work. One of their favorite sports was coursing the bull, which they called *corrida de toro.* A lively bull was let loose within a fenced arena, and mounted men waved capes or *serapes* at him until he charged. He was chased by all the riders, each one trying to *colear el toro,* to grasp his tail and give it a twist that would dump him to the ground.

Another game the *Californios* played was to rope a grizzly bear—three or four vaqueros worked together to get several lariats onto a big one—and then to match the bear in a gory, eye-popping fight with the strongest, fiercest bull rounded up at the rodeo. Horse racing and roping contests were popular sports, and there were various riding tricks. One required a horseman to lean low from the saddle while riding at top speed and scoop up a coin from the ground. In another, a coin was placed beneath each knee of the rider, who then galloped and jumped his mount over several hurdles and, returning over the same course, wove in and out among the hurdles to halt before a judge who checked to see that the coins were still in place.

A live rooster was roughly used in a game called *el carrera del gallo*. The bird was buried in the dirt with only his head showing. Starting from two hundred feet away, a vaquero spurred to a gallop, and as he rode by, leaned from the saddle and tried to grab the rooster by the neck and pull him free.

But life had not been all fun and games for the mission Indians. For them it consisted mainly of work and prayer, and of punishments for laziness or for trying to run away. In the 1820's most of the natives in the coastal area lived in or near the missions, but few were entirely content with their lot. They were virtually slaves, and although docile, they had to be kept under strict control by their masters. In 1833 the Mexican government declared the mission lands open to settlers and released the Indians from mission control. Finding themselves suddenly free, the Indians responded with violence. After a wild round of looting and destruction, during which thousands of cattle were slaughtered, most of them fled to the hills and resumed their former way of life. Others became peons on the great ranchos, where they were never paid.

At San Gabriel Mission thirty thousand animals had been put to death by the Indians for the mere joy of killing, and for the next few years the bleached bones of the great mission herds were used by settlers for building mile after mile of fences.

Life on the great California ranches could be dull because of the great distances between neighbors; the rancheros and vaqueros, therefore, participated in violent sports to pass the time. The vaqueros above have roped a bear that they will use in a fight with a bull. The brave young California woman on horseback (below) is participating in the ancient Spanish sport of bull-baiting.

The Spanish never found gold in California, although they lived near it and over it. On January 24, 1848, an American carpenter named Marshall discovered gold at Sutter's Mill near Sacramento, and on February 2, 1848, California was ceded to the United States as a result of the Mexican War. The charming, gay life of the *Californios* was over. When the great hordes of men swarmed into the gold fields in 1849, the demand for beef depleted what was left of the California herds. And soon the influx of settlers changed the very character of the land; it was divided into smaller parcels; the ranges and the herds disappeared, and the open range became farm land.

Enterprising Texans began to take advantage of this situation by trailing their longhorns all the way from Texas to the coastal meadows of California. The trail was long and beset by hostile Indians, but a Texan named Trimmier demonstrated that it was worth attempting when he drove five hundred longhorns through to the gold fields and sold them at one hundred dollars a head. Riding back toward Texas, Trimmier met other herds, swinging along westward.

Eventually there were several well-traveled routes from Texas to California. Some of the California-bound drovers followed a long route that went up the Rio Grande, crossed the Continental Divide in Colorado, trended northwest to the Overland Trail, and then headed across Nevada's

alkali flats into California and thence to San Francisco. It was an arduous, punishing drive, but most of those who started it made it to their destination. Those who followed more southerly routes crossed the Rio Grande near Albuquerque, went through northern Arizona, up along the rugged eastern slopes of the Sierra Nevada (called by trail drivers "the Elephant") and through a pass that led into California. Others, after crossing southern New Mexico, followed the Gila River to the Yuma crossing of the Colorado, then proceeded on to Los Angeles and north to the gold camps.

Texas cattle continued to supply much of California's beef diet until the outbreak of the Civil War. The terrible risks were offset by the high profits—cattle that could be bought in Texas for anywhere from five dollars to fifteen dollars a head would bring prices of from $25 to $150 in the Pacific Coast markets. For that much promise, enterprising ex-soldiers from the Texas Revolution and the Mexican War were ready to fight off whooping raiders, and endure choking dust, scorching winds, drought-tindered grass, alkali water, poison weeds, and hoof-cutting rocks.

The *Californios* did not exert a lasting influence on the cattle industry. But the long drives taught the Texans that their herds could be driven, against almost impossible odds, to a market, instead of waiting for the market to come to them—a forecast of the great cattle drives to come.

TERMS USED BY MEXICAN COWBOYS

ARMAS: skins attached to the pommel of a saddle to protect the legs from brush and thorns.

BRASADA: brush country — a region covered with thickets.

CALIFORNIO: a Spanish Californian.

EL CARRERA DEL GALLO: coursing the rooster.

CIMARRONES: wild cattle.

COLEAR EL TORO: to throw a bull by grabbing his tail and giving it a twist.

CORRIDA DE TORO: baiting the bull.

DAR LA VUELTA: dolly welter — to wrap a rope around the pommel instead of tying; to dolly or dally a rope.

FANDANGO: a dance, an entertainment with dancing.

MATANZA: a slaughtering of animals.

MESTEÑOS: strayed or wild cattle and horses — mustangs.

RANCHERO: rancher.

REATA: rawhide rope used by the vaqueros — lariat.

REMUDA: relay of horses.

VAQUERO: mounted herdsman, Spanish cowboy, buckaroo.

The vaquero (below center), reaching down from his galloping horse to pull a partially buried rooster from the ground, is a contestant in el carrera del gallo. This favorite sport required the sort of expert horsemanship that only the bravest vaqueros could achieve.

1840 South side M[...]

The
Long Drives
Begin

Plaza san Antonio Texas

San Antonio's main plaza (above), with its thick-walled adobe buildings (in the background), still looked like the center of a typically Mexican town in 1849 when this picture was painted by the local sheriff. By this time, however, San Antonio was one of the most important cattle towns in the American Southwest and was the scene of much cattle trading and selling.

In 1843, an Englishman, William Bollaert, visited San Antonio, Texas. He saw a new kind of American, "a rude uncultivated race of beings, who pass the greater part of their lives in the saddle, herding cattle and horses, and in hunting deer, buffalo, or mustangs [wild cattle]. Unused to comfort, and regardless alike of ease and danger, they have a hardy, brigand, sunburnt appearance . . . with a slouched hat, leather hunting shirt, leggings and Indian moccasins, armed with a large knife, musket, or rifle, and sometimes pistols."

South from the Nueces to the Rio Grande, sweeping east to the Gulf of Mexico, stretched the brasada—the defiant brush country. Hot, hazy with gray dust, blistered by winds, its interlocking miles of mesquite, cat's-claw, and thorny thickets furnished a hiding place for millions of wild cattle that were descended from those first Spanish herds and from the loose cattle that had drifted away from the Mexican ranchos broken up after the Texas Revolution of 1836. Here was the cradle and breeding ground for the Texas longhorn. Frank Dobie says, in *The Longhorns,* that "the way to make cattle wild is to turn them loose in the wilderness and chase them." This, over years of border warfare and Indian raiding, was what had happened in the brasada.

Texas was estimated to have had 100,000 wild cattle in 1830; by 1850, 330,000; and in 1860, more than 3,500,000. Some experts said there were even more. The protective wild country, and the stamina and fighting qualities of the animals allowed them to multiply to the extent that they were considered either as a great source of wealth or as dangerous pests, depending on the point of view. Colonel Richard I. Dodge, in *Hunting Grounds of the Great West,* writing of his experiences in the early fifties said, "the domestic cattle of Texas, miscalled tame, are fifty times more dangerous to footmen than the fiercest buffalo . . . the wild bull is 'on his muscle' at all times; and although he will generally get out of the way if unmolested, the slightest provocation will convert him into a most aggressive and dangerous enemy." The *mesteños* could be caught and after a few days of penning, herded, but the wildest, the *cimarrones,* if caught, often died in captivity.

The men who caught them had taken up this occupation as a result of war. Thousands of American volunteers had flocked into Texas during the revolution. After the Battle of San Jacinto, when Santa Anna's Mexican army was pushed back across the Rio Grande, groups of these young men drifted down into the brasada. In order to survive in Texas, they had learned, through bitter experience with the Comanche and Mexicans, to fight without quarter, to ride as well as their enemies, and to shoot better than either of them. Armed with six-shooters, the pistols invented by Samuel Colt and first used by the Texas Rangers in 1839, the Texans could shoot six times from the saddle without reloading. (In 1850, Captain I. S. Sutton of the Rangers wrote that the "six-shooter is the arm which has rendered the name of Texas Ranger a check and terror to the bands of our frontier Indians.")

Mexican ranchers, the former inhabitants of the brasada, had fled back south of the Rio Grande. Even their branded cattle now roamed free. The young cow hunters recognized no rights of the Mexicans. Cattle were there for the taking, and the Texans meant to take them. They hunted in groups, chasing the animals into pens where they were kept until there was a herd large enough to drive north. The hunters began to earn a name from their activity—cowboy, an old term applied during the American Revolution to Tory snipers who hid in

Comanche Indians on the trail (above) were a fearful sight for the cattle ranchers of the Great Plains. The ranchers knew that the fierce, warlike tribe considered them and their herds trespassers on Comanche land.

The two vaqueros below are slaughtering a steer outside the ranch house. The man at right will cut the animal's throat with a knife; it is quite likely that this steer had been intended for use as food on the ranch.

thickets and jingled cowbells to lure the patriots within their gun range. A man called Ewen Cameron was the best known leader of the Texas cow hunters, so they were widely known as "Cameron's Cowboys." Ewen Cameron has sometimes been called the first cowboy.

For some time, the term cowboy carried a derogatory meaning. Cowboys were rough and ready operators, but the country and the cattle were even wilder. Cow hunting was as unsuited to the gentle spirited as it was to the fainthearted.

From the brasada, the cowboys drove their newly acquired stock north at a hard run toward the safe timber country of the Brazos River in eastern Texas — the well-watered, lush land where the Apache and Comanche were not in the habit of raiding; there the pace could be slackened.

Some of the cattle were driven clear to New Orleans and sold there, but more were kept in the coastal regions to be used in stocking east Texas ranches. Trading in this "imported" stock centered in the old town of Goliad on the San Antonio River.

In the 1830's, Texans who owned broad pastures had had relatively few cattle; they were more interested in acquiring stock than in selling it. But during the next decade or so their "cow critters" bred and multiplied, and by the 1840's men owned great herds and were beginning to look for more grass —and for markets that wanted large quantities of beef.

There were precedents for trail-driving cattle to far-off markets by now. A few drives had been made to Louisiana when Texas was under foreign rule—first under Spain, then under Mexico. In 1838, James White, who owned a ranch on Galveston Bay, trailed a herd through the bayou country to the Mississippi River. Others brought herds along this route to Louisiana markets during the next few years; and starting in 1842, Texas cattle were regularly trailed to New Orleans.

Even earlier, up in the North, drovers had begun gathering large herds of cattle to trail them east to Ohio, and sometimes farther. Benjamin Harris took several herds east from Illinois, swimming the Wabash River and driving on to Pennsylvania and Maryland. In 1845, John T. Alexander—who later became the country's foremost cattle shipper—drove 250 head all the way from Illinois to Boston.

The West's first great cattle drive took place on the Pacific Coast in 1837. Ewing Young, a fur trapper who knew the mountain trails from Canada to Mexico, led a small group of French-Canadians and Americans from Oregon's Willamette Valley settlement to California. There they bought eight hundred head of half-wild cattle described as "blood cousins to the Texas longhorns of a later era," to deliver to the hard-up Yankees in disputed Oregon Territory. It was a terrible journey north. After taking a maddening month to get the unruly herd across the San Joaquin River, Young and his men pushed the cattle through a maze of ridges, ravines, and tangled brush. There was a running, three-day fight with Rogue River Indians near the end of the drive. In all, it took nineteen weeks to cover the seven hundred miles; but the remaining 630 cattle did wonders for the morale of the Willamette colonists.

The Oregon Trail also had its share of cattle drives. The best known of these was part of the Indian missionary Marcus Whitman's Great Emigration in 1843. Some sixty owner-drivers, under the leadership of Jesse Apple-

gate, herded more than three thousand head of choice stock from the Kansas River, near present Topeka, to Fort Walla Walla—a bone-wearing two thousand miles—in about six months. Applegate, a lean Kentuckian "so homely he avoided mirrors all his life," was a man of great character and personal force whose achievement was one of the most significant in frontier history.

The first big drive north from Texas on record was made in 1846, when Edward Piper trailed a thousand head to Ohio, but it was not destined to stand as a unique achievement for very

In the 1830's when this drawing was made, Independence, Missouri (below), was the busy eastern terminus of the famous Santa Fe Trail. In the 1850's Independence became an important market for cattle driven north from Texas.

long. More and more longhorns were being delivered to points north of Indian Territory (now Oklahoma) during the 1850's. A route familiar to Indians, traders, and pioneers for many years furnished a ready-made trail. The Texas-bound settlers who had ridden over it called it the Texas Road; to the drovers who used it later it was, at first, simply the "cattle trail," later, the Kansas Trail. The name Shawnee Trail, which it eventually acquired, probably was derived from the Indian village of Shawneetown, on the Red River near the place where the trail crossed the river.

North of the Red River, the trail went through Choctaw Indian country, passed Fort Washita (established in 1842 to offer the Chickasaw and Choctaw protection against the hostile Plains tribes), crossed the Canadian River and Creek Indian territory, then the Arkansas; went by Fort Gibson, one of the oldest frontier outposts; and passed through the lands of the Cherokee, to cut across the southeastern corner of Kansas before swinging northeast to the Missouri River and St. Louis.

Kansas and Missouri farmers and cattle raisers were literally up in arms to express their resistance to the cattle drives. They feared the cattle ticks that clung to the Texas longhorns for hundreds of miles, then dropped off and caused disastrous outbreaks of "Texas fever" among the domestic stock, which lacked the apparent immunity that protected the longhorns. The two states involved passed laws to prevent the passage of Texas herds, and when the drives kept on coming through, the determined local inhab-

itants took drastic steps and set up an effective "shotgun quarantine."

Still, some of the more stubborn Texans continued to drive north and managed to get cattle through. The incidence of the fever lessened in 1859 and 1860, and traffic on the trail picked up considerably. In May, 1859, a Dallas newspaper reported the pasage of a large herd "en route for the North, to feed our abolition neighbors. We hope that southern diet may agree with them."

By 1854, a year when fifty thousand longhorns were reported to have crossed the Red River bound for the northern markets, the Shawnee Trail was established as an important cattle route. Many of the trailsmen, after leaving Indian Territory, were now taking their herds straight north to Kansas City, Westport, and Independence, instead of driving to St. Louis. These towns offered ready markets; here westbound freighters and pioneers heading for California and Oregon were fitting out; army quartermasters and Indian agents were buying beeves; and midwestern cattle dealers were taking on Texas steers to fatten and ship to the East.

It was inevitable that some of the cattle from the Trinity and the Brazos rivers eventually should reach New York City. The great port city saw its first Texas longhorns in 1854. A young midwesterner, Tom Candy Ponting, and his partner, Washington Malone, in 1853 had ridden to Texas, where they bought seven hundred head and trailed them to Illinois, where they were kept through the winter. The following summer, a hundred and fifty of them were driven to Muncie, Indiana, shipped by railroad to New York, and sold, at Fourth Avenue and Forty-fourth Street, bringing a good price.

Tom Candy Ponting eventually published the story of his 1853 drive. "We crossed into Missouri out of the Indian country, near what is now known as Baxter Springs," he wrote. "I sat on my horse every night while we were coming through the Indian country; I was so afraid that something would scare the cattle that I could not sleep in the tent; but we had no stampede. When we got into Missouri . . . we held our

cattle about three miles southwest of Springfield until we got things straightened up. . . . We had to depend on long drives until we got to St. Louis. . . . Had to make several stops while crossing [the Mississippi by ferry]. We had hard work to keep the cattle from plunging into the river. On the other side of the river, where East St. Louis now is, the country was very open and we had plenty of grass. . . . We camped here and this was the end of our travels, for we wintered in this country. . . . We kept some [of the cattle] on feed for fattening, and others we put out in different bunches to be fed for the winter on rough feed."

Those specially fattened steers of Ponting's were shipped by rail to New York the next year. All told, about

750 longhorn beeves from Texas herds reached the metropolis in 1855.

The longhorns failed to win ready acceptance by the New Yorkers. One of the city's newspapers commented sourly that they were "barely able to cast a shadow" and "would not weigh anything were it not for their horns, which were useful also in preventing them from crawling through fences."

Actually, most of the Texas cattle that reached the city had horns of moderate length. One of the herds got out of control and ran loose on the street after delivery; it would have rated as a mild run in Texas or on the trail, but no doubt those horns looked ten feet long to the New Yorkers.

But now the continuation of the northward trek was threatened by something more ominous than conflict over Texas fever and hard trailing. When the guns at Fort Sumter signaled the opening of the Civil War, they also sounded the death knell for the long-distance cattle trade. President Lincoln's order forbidding all trade with the South was followed by one to blockade the Confederacy's coasts.

Except for a few men who dared to seek profit by trading with the enemy, the Texans lost their market outlets in the North for the duration of the war. Most able-bodied Texans old enough

The two cowboys at left are beginning to "cut out" a herd (divide it into smaller groups of cattle) during a big roundup. This job, which had to be done cautiously to avoid a stampede, required the very best horses.

to bear arms went off to fight for the Southern cause. Range operations were neglected; herds began to scatter and wander back into the brush. Still, with the Confederate commissaries seeking supplies and offering fair prices, some older stockmen and beardless Texas youths contrived to gather herds and trail them through to feed the gray-clad forces. John ("Jinglebob") Chisum and his men drove longhorns down the Red River valley to Shreveport. Chisum, who ran the largest ranch in Texas before the Civil War, was called "Jinglebob John" and "Boss of the Jinglebob" because the earmark he put on his cattle split the ears so that the lower part dangled limply—(earmarks were used as well as brands to show who owned cattle). Oliver Loving also delivered several herds to the Rebel soldiers east of the Mississippi, and other Texans trailed beef on the hoof to New Orleans during the first year of the war.

In October, 1862, Jim Borroum and Monroe Choate set out to drive eight hundred head from Goliad to New Orleans. One of their trail hands was a slim boy of seventeen named W. D. H. Saunders. They knew that the soldiers in Louisiana needed beef, and they were determined to get it to them. The herd was scattered in a wild stampede as they passed through Lavaca County, but young Saunders and his friends patiently rounded them up again and went on. They swam the Colorado, the Brazos, the Trinity, the Neches, the Sabine.

The vaqueros in this painting are roping a spirited bull that had probably strayed from the herd. The reatas, or catch ropes, that the vaqueros used so expertly were usually made of rope or of greased rawhide.

A cavalry detachment rode up to them one day in Louisiana, and the Texans were much relieved to find that the horsemen were Confederates.

The officer at their head asked the drovers where they were going. Young Saunders and the others told him with a sense of importance and pride, that they were taking the beeves to New Orleans. Unbeknown to them the city had been in the hands of Union forces for several months. The officer was unwilling to believe they were ignorant of the fact, and the bewildered Texans found themselves under arrest for trying to aid the enemy!

Fortunately for them the officer who presided at their trial was convinced of their innocence. He released them and advised them to stay far north of New Orleans. They decided that it would be safe to strike out for Mobile, which was still Rebel controlled. It was a long way off, and on the far side of the Mississippi, but they were undaunted.

A few days later they halted on the west bank of the mighty river. It was a mile wide, and forty feet deep. There were no ferries. One of the youths rode his horse into the water. Soon his mount was swimming as he headed for that far-off east bank. The others, yipping and slapping their coiled lariats, urged the nervous longhorns into the stream.

About a hundred of the cattle balked and would not take the water, but the end result was a near-miracle: all the rest clambered out, dripping and

John Chisum

weary, on the far shore. Jubilant, the Texans drove their "sea lions" north along the river heading for Woodville, Mississippi.

Their troubles had not ended, though. They ran into another group of Confederate horsemen and again they were taken into custody. This time they were confined for several days before a rebel military court released them. Resuming their drive,

Charles Goodnight

Oliver Loving

Jesse Chisholm

The early cattle industry of Texas produced men who were both bold frontiersmen and good businessmen. Chisum had become the biggest cattleman in Texas by 1861. He drove his herds to the railroad over a series of trails called the Chisum Trails (see the map on page 62). Goodnight and Loving started their careers as trail drivers; they established the Goodnight-Loving Trail to New Mexico. Loving, who is also credited with starting the Shawnee Trail, died in 1867 from wounds received in an Indian attack on a herd he was driving. Jesse Chisholm, an Indian scout, established the Chisholm Trail in 1865. Samuel Maverick, a Texas rancher, gave his name to maverick (unbranded) cattle. It is said that one of his hands neglected to brand some of his cattle and his neighbors came to call all unbranded cattle "one of Maverick's."

Samuel Maverick

they reached Woodville, where to their relief they were able to sell the herd.

It was a tremendous achievement, but an experience that might have dimmed the loyalty of some for the Southern cause. Such was not the case with young W. D. H. Saunders, however. He made his way back to Goliad, and early in 1863 he enlisted in the Confederate Army.

While Texas men were away from home fighting, the herds of longhorn cattle, largely neglected, prospered and multiplied. The bulls remained uncastrated, and their numbers forced them into the wild pattern of fighting for the cows; the result was wilder animals and greatly increased herds. By the summer of 1865, some six million of them were roaming the unfenced range lands and wilderness of southwest Texas.

The Great Trails

Among the detachments of troops that Texas sent to fight for the Confederacy during the Civil War was Terry's Texas Rangers (officially called the Eighth Texas Cavalry); four members of this hard-riding group are shown above. The man brandishing a canteen above his head is Samuel Maverick, the cattleman.

For Texans, the main task when the Civil War ended was the stark and simple one of economic survival. The people of the Lone-Star State were broke. Paper currency that had been issued under Jefferson Davis was now worthless. The bonds that the Southern states had sold were repudiated. Gold and silver coins were almost as scarce as two-headed calves. The outlook was bleak. Still, there were the longhorns—more beef on the hoof than the Texans could eat. Here was one asset that might be turned into good hard cash if the animal could be gotten to market.

The problem was that the northern markets were a long way off. It would take time and hard work to get the cattle there, but these Texans had plenty of time, and there was an old range saying that nobody ever drowned himself in sweat.

So the Texans, men and boys, many still in ragged coats they had worn while riding or marching for Lee or Jackson or Hood, set to work. They searched the brush and combed the draws (gullies) and rode the range from dawn to dark, rounding up cattle —"making the gather." Many of the tame herds were scattered, gone half-wild, and were running with the brush-ranging *cimarrones*. All of them, including the sure-footed, twisty-horned brutes that lurked in the tangled thickets and wooded creek bottoms, were hunted down by the lean and purposeful saddle men.

Once caught, the longhorns were

thrown together in herds of from two to three thousand head for the long trip up the trail. There were not many ranchers who could scour out that many critters worth driving north, even counting the wild ones that were getting their first taste of men with ropes and branding irons. So the ranchers banded together, threw their cattle, or "stuff," into a trail herd, and chose one of their number to boss the operation. To him, they turned over bills of sale for their own animals, getting his note in return, or, more likely, his word. He would direct the drive, give orders to the riders who went with him, deliver the beeves at the end of the trail, and bring back the money.

Sometimes mixed herds—"she stuff" (cows), steers (castrated males), and bulls—were headed up the trail. Some drivers preferred to concentrate on steers, which were better walkers, although less placid and more likely to panic and run. Four-year-olds were considered best for the beef markets; but younger animals were often included.

The Texans knew what paths led to the markets or railroad shipping points in Missouri and eastern Kansas. Some of them had been up the trail before the war began, when they had used the route that came to be called the Shawnee Trail.

That trail led through hilly, wooded country, with deep, steep-banked streams. It was not an easy region to drive through. In addition to the physical difficulties, the Choctaw Indians

had become stock raisers themselves, and they objected to Texas herds being driven through their lands while they were trying to gather their own cattle after the confusion of the war.

Jim Daugherty was only nineteen when, in 1866, he bought five hundred steers to drive north over the Shawnee Trail; but he had already learned a lot about handling cattle. Having hired five cowboys to help him, he crossed the Red River with his herd and headed for Baxter Springs. He planned to drive his steers on from there to Sedalia, Missouri, which the Missouri-Pacific Railroad had reached a few years before. There he could load his cattle on the cars for St. Louis—but the roads to Sedalia were dangerous to drive. Attracted by the increased activity in the area, the most vicious of the western postwar cattle thieves infested these roads. They pirated cattle, stampeded them at night, and often murdered to steal the trailing herds.

There were also constant threats from the Kansas farmers who feared the "Texas fever" spread by the ticks which infested the longhorns from the southern ranges. That fear was used as an excuse by bands of Jayhawkers to plunder the Texans' herds. (Before the Civil War, the Jayhawkers had

In the illustration at right, taken from a history of the cattle trade published in 1874, a cattleman is suffering the same fate at the hands of a band of Jayhawkers that Jim Daugherty suffered. An outlaw (background) stampedes the herd while its driver is beaten.

been free-soil partisans who fought against the proslavery bushwhacker bands of Missouri in the border strife connected with the settlement of Kansas Territory.)

Whether because of careful driving or good fortune, Jim Daugherty got through Indian Territory without any losses or stampedes, stream crossings, or redskins; but as he rode ahead of his herd toward Baxter Springs he picked up news of trouble ahead. An outlaw gang had killed one drover and scattered his cattle. Other trail bosses were holding their herds on the grass, uncertain about going ahead. Jim let his trail hands stay with his steers while he rode along to Fort Scott, a town north of Baxter Springs, and made an agreement to sell his stock.

He and his men drove the five hundred head north along the Kansas-Missouri border. They tried to keep alert for trouble, but they were caught by surprise when a score of border ruffians whooped down on them, shot one of Jim's riders dead, and stampeded the cattle.

Covered by guns, Daugherty was ordered to dismount. Then the raiders

tied him to a tree and gave him a brutal flogging. They charged him with driving diseased cattle through their territory. They would not let him defend himself, and they refused to examine the cattle. Somebody yelled, "Hang him!" But Jim Daugherty looked so young; perhaps that stirred compassion in some of them, for they decided to let him go.

Freed, Jim located the rest of his men, and together they rounded up all the steers they could. About a hundred and fifty were gone for good. After they had buried their dead comrade, Jim located a guide who knew the country intimately, and with his help, driving by night, Jim and his men got the remainder of the herd to Fort Scott. There Jim sold the steers for a profit, in spite of the fact that he had lost thirty per cent of his original herd.

Other Texans who came up the trail in that year of 1866 also ran into trouble. One had his herd turned back at the Missouri border by a band of hard-eyed men armed with guns. He drove his cattle back to the Arkansas line, and trailed them clear to the Mississippi River, finally crossing at St. Louis. By that time they were so trail-gaunted that he had to corn-feed them before trying to sell them to Illinois farmers.

While many of the Texas trailsmen were holding their herds around Baxter Springs, hoping that conditions

A cowboy's life during a long cattle drive was often unpleasant. Breaking camp in the morning on a wet, cold day (below) was discouraging for men who had slept outside all night and faced a hard day's work ahead.

would improve, hard, early frosts killed the grass, and with feed scarce, many cattle died. Some of the bosses had to sell their stock at a loss.

Not all the trail drivers looked to the north. Thirty-year-old Charlie Goodnight, who ran cattle along the Brazos, in the Palo Pinto region of north-central Texas, judged that Colorado would offer a good market for his stock.

Goodnight talked with his neighbors about trailing southwest to the Pecos River, which could then be followed up into New Mexico and Colorado; but they shook their heads and frowned—what about that dry stretch this side of the Pecos? They all shook their heads, except one older man, Oliver Loving, who—before the Civil War—had trailed Texas cattle to Louisiana and Illinois and, once, even to Denver, by driving them north to the Arkansas River, then following its course westward.

In 1866 the two men gathered a mixed herd of steers, cows, and calves, numbering two thousand head, and set out. They took eighteen well-armed men with them. Goodnight, the younger man, rode ahead to scout for grass and water and keep a lookout for Comanche; Loving, older and trailwise, stuck with the herd.

Things went smoothly at first. Oppressive heat, blinding dust, and the bawling of cows whose newly dropped calves had to be killed because they couldn't keep up were all things that had been expected. Then they reached the jumping-off place; ahead of them was the eighty-mile waterless stretch they had to cross to reach the Pecos. Twelve to fifteen miles was reckoned a long enough drive under the hot sun from one watering place to the next. So they made a long stop at the head of Middle Concho, letting the stock drink all they wanted, while the men filled their canteens and water barrels.

Then Oliver Loving and Charlie Goodnight and their eighteen cowboys and their two thousand cattle left the Middle Concho. They were heading for Horsehead Crossing, eighty miles to the west, which was the first reasonably safe ford on the Pecos River north of the Rio Grande, and the crucial spot on the new cattle trail.

It was afternoon when they set out, the sun already low. They drove late into the evening, made camp, bedding the stock down in the dark, and then hit saddles for an early start. That day gave cattle, horses, and men a taste of what was to come. When night fell, the thirsty herd would not bed down, but milled around so it was hard to hold them. Before dawn, the herd was headed out again.

That second full day, the animals tried to break and head back for the last remembered water. Weaker ones that hung behind had to be whipped on, while a few strong leaders, swinging along too fast, were held back only by constant effort. Canteens were emptied. The water in the barrels went down. Wild-eyed critters bawled and moaned; their tongues hung out, coat-

These galloping cowboys are making a dash for a wooded area in order to escape a party of Indians. Plains Indians, not accustomed to fighting among the trees, tried not to enter the timber.

Sedalia, Missouri (1866)

Abilene, Kansas (c. 1870)

ed with dust. Riders' lips cracked; reddened eyes stung, and the lids puffed and burned. Loving, using all his hard-earned trail wisdom, worked tirelessly at the drag, determined to save every dumb brute he could, as disaster loomed beside him.

Through another night they plodded on, the near-exhausted riders and stumble-footed stock following the bell sounds that came from the lead steers. The next day men were slumping, almost helpless, in their saddles. One of them collapsed, and he was left in the shade of an arroyo bank, with part of a canteen of water and instructions to follow the trail after the sun had set.

Animals were dropping and men were clinging desperately to their mounts when Goodnight, loaded with empty canteens, set out at a fast pace to ride ahead to the river. When he got back to the herd again, Pecos water sloshing in those canteens, he saw at once that the situation was desperate. The weakest would have to be sacrificed to save the rest, he decided. He picked the horses and men who seemed to be in the best shape. They headed the stronger cattle for the Pecos, letting them go as fast as they could. Loving and the other riders kept the rest of the stock traveling at a slower pace.

When, finally, the lead animals in Goodnight's bunch smelled Pecos water they ran as fast as their trembling legs would carry them. The handful of men tried desperately to keep the other cattle strung out behind them; for, the moment they sensed the change and followed excitedly after the leaders, they would pile together, bunched, into the river. The men failed: the animals that crowded from the rear pushed the leaders across the river and out of the water before they could drink. The bawling, frantic herd spread out both ways in the narrow stream, to make a living dam. When Loving's men got the weaker stock near, they went over a high bank in a wild run. A hundred drowned or were lost in quicksand, adding their toll to the three hundred others that had expired on the way.

Dodge City, Kansas (1878)

After the Civil War, when the great cattle drives occurred in increasing numbers, cow towns grew up quickly at the ends of the trails. In these towns, the western cattle were sold and shipped east by means of the rapidly expanding railroad system. The three towns at left were extremely important market centers which, only a few years before these photographs were taken, had been sleepy frontier towns. Abilene, one of the most important and crowded of all of the cow towns, had ten boarding houses, 32 saloons, five general stores, and four hotels by 1870.

45

Finally they got the herd under control, and after several days of grazing and resting, the partners pushed on to Fort Sumner, where they sold the steers. Loving trailed the cows and calves on into Colorado, disposing of them there, while Goodnight hurried back to the Brazos, carrying $12,000 in gold, to buy another herd. This time he got nothing but steers and, following the trail so recently made, brought them from the Middle Concho to the Pecos without losing a head.

It was a notable feat, and the route so courageously laid out by the partners was justly named the Goodnight-Loving Trail. It was fairly popular as a route to market for a while, but it was not long before the Comanche learned that valuable meat on the hoof was being driven along this way regularly, and began to pay it their vicious brand of attention. A raiding band even managed to trap canny old Oliver Loving, "Dean of the Trail Drivers." He was wounded, and three weeks later he died of gangrene. At his request Goodnight took his body back to Texas.

However, the achievements of Goodnight and Loving, dramatic and colorful as they were, proved but side eddies in the main stream of the growing cattle-trail trade. Texan supply and

Yankee demand were to get together for the first time really effectively when Joseph G. McCoy, a shrewd cattle broker from Illinois, built extensive corrals at the Kansas town of Abilene, until then a shack town whose main industry was catching prairie dogs. He persuaded a railroad company to load beef cattle there for the Chicago stockyards. McCoy then dispatched agents to spread the word among the northbound cattle drovers of the advantages offered by Abilene: ample pens and

Not everyone in Texas worked at ranching. The peaceful farm at right was located in the lush country of east Texas at the time of the Civil War. Although the farmers of Texas were not likely to make as much money as cattlemen, they did lead calmer lives.

holding grounds, guaranteed car service, freedom from the armed farmers and Jayhawkers of eastern Kansas.

McCoy's advertising was effective; in 1869, Abilene's second full season, some 150,000 longhorns were delivered to the town. Most of them came north to Abilene by a route that came to be called the Chisholm Trail, one of the most widely publicized and best known roads in history. It got its name from a half-breed Indian trader, Jesse Chisholm, who had driven his goods wagon along it, between Wichita, Kansas, and the Washita River market in Indian Territory. From the latter point, the trail ran south some eighty miles to Red River Station, which was about one hundred miles west of Colbert's Ferry, the principal crossing used by drovers on the old Shawnee Trail. Feeder lines from most of the ranges of east and central Texas led into the Chisholm Trail.

Cattle flowed along the Chisholm in great quantity for several years; still,

it was not free of hazards. The Chickasaw, through whose lands it ran, levied a grazing tax of as much as fifty cents a head on all stock being trailed through. Farmers, pushing ever westward, began to show up and make trouble with their fences. The old "Texas fever" charge was flung at the trailsmen again; the quarantine lines showed up once more—behind them the grim settlers with guns cocked.

Gradually, the trail outfits began to swing farther west, their herds merging with others originating farther west in Texas. Simultaneously, new shipping facilities were being built on the railroad tracks that crossed the state of Kansas—at Ellsworth, at Newton, and finally, at Dodge City.

Dodge City, the greatest, most colorful, brawling, and lawless of all the trail-end towns, became the terminal

point of the Western (or Dodge City) Trail, which, starting north from Fort Griffin, Texas, spanned the Red River at Doan's Crossing, traversed the Indian Territory and its great rivers, to come to the Arkansas, on the northern bank of which Dodge City perched.

The trail went through country that was roamed by proud, fierce, fight-minded warriors—Comanche, Kiowa, Cheyenne, Arapaho—who would

The herd shown below in a photograph taken around 1910 on the Matador Range of Texas is being driven slowly toward the railroad at Lubbock, Texas. By 1910 the use of railroads for shipping cattle was a firmly established practice; the days of the great trail drives were long past, and short drives like the one in this photograph were common.

rather collect scalps than collect the tolls exacted by their more civilized racial fellows to the east. In spite of their attentions, though, the drovers managed to get through to Dodge with both their scalps and their herds. Or most of them did, anyway.

The name of Dodge City still stands for long-horned cattle and trail drivers with sun-squinted eyes, after the long trek through a wild, uncurried country, riding boldly into town to "turn loose." Captain Henry King of Kansas wrote, "the town rubbed its eyes . . . and leaped to its feet . . . glasses clinked, dice rattled . . . violins, flutes, and cor-

nets sent eager strains of waltz and polka . . . And everywhere stared and shone the Lone Star of Texas. As the night sped on . . . the saloons became clamorous with ribald songs and laughter. At length, as we looked and listened, the sharp, significant report of a pistol . . ."

Eventually other towns sprang up out of nowhere as the great Western Trail reached north to Ogallala, Nebraska, and on into Dakota Territory, but none of them ever approached the notoriety of Dodge, wildest of the rip-roaring frontier towns, where cowboys cut loose after the long drives.

The scenes at left and below would seem quite familiar to a cowboy who had participated in the West's great trail drives. The picture at left shows the herd on the trail with cowboys riding behind it and on its flanks. Trail drivers had to be constantly on the alert for steers straying from the herd—for one steer could start a stampede that might cause the loss of many head of cattle. In the picture below, the herd is shown as it is watered in a stream near the trail. The water stops provided both the cowboys and the cattle with a much needed change from the boredom of their journey. The cowboys, however, had to watch the herd carefully for signs of panic— even at the most peaceful streams.

Life
on the Trail

About thirty-five thousand men took part in the great cattle drives that were made after the Civil War, and probably about one third of these men were Mexicans and Negroes. Many guesses have been made as to the number of Texas cattle that went up the trails to market and to the ranges in the north during this period. George W. Saunders, who organized the Trail Drivers of Texas, and Charlie Goodnight figured that by 1895 some ten thousand cattle and about one million horses left Texas by way of the trails.

The size of a trail herd depended on circumstances. The sheer difficulty of controlling vast numbers of animals on the trail and the tasks of watering them and bedding them down at night were limiting factors.

In 1884, Walter Billingsley brought a big herd of King Ranch cattle to Dodge City and there combined it with another large one to continue on to Montana; together they made a herd of 5,600 head, big enough to keep cattlemen talking for a long time. The record seems to have been set in 1869 by another group of Texans; starting from the Brazos River, they lined out a herd of fifteen thousand cattle for California. The outfit included two hundred peo-

ple, well over a thousand horses, and a great number of wagons. The cattle were driven in four separate bunches but were bedded together whenever there was danger of a night attack by Indians.

Preparing for a trail drive took careful planning. Early in the spring, the drover—either a rancher or an enterprising cattle buyer—set out to gather a trail herd. If he was a buyer, he might visit several ranches and make arrangements for cattle to be delivered to a central place where the herd was to be made up. There the cattle were given a special brand for the drive—the pur-

The cowboy above, trying to relax on his horse, is riding day herd on the cattle as they graze slowly on their northward course. Although it was often hot and dusty on day herd, many cowboys preferred this duty to the lonely hours of riding night herd.

pose of this road-brand being to show change of ownership and prevent confusion or misunderstanding as the herd went up the trail.

A trail boss was hired to guide and control the herd until it reached its destination. He might be paid as much as $125 a month—high wages for those times, but he was in complete charge of men, equipment, and animals representing an investment of many thousands of dollars. The cowboys who worked the herd were paid from $25 to $40 a month. There was also a cook, usually an older man than the cowboys; his pay, somewhat higher than theirs, was well earned: he sometimes rolled out of his blankets to start making breakfast at three o'clock in the morning, and sometimes would not be ready to hit them again until near midnight. Nor could he afford to doze much while driving the chuck wagon —a job he handled in addition to preparing the meals—at least, not while they were driving through Indian country. Usually the chuck wagon preceded the herd and the cowboys by a mile or more, so the cook was more or less on his own.

A trail outfit was rounded out with a wrangler, whose job was to take care of the horse herd—variously called *caballada*, *remuda*, or saddle band— and the riding equipment. As a rule, the wrangler was the youngest of all the trail hands, sometimes a boy on his first drive, who drew less pay than the others. *Remudas* ranged in size from just two or three horses for each rider to as many as six. A cowboy saved his best horse for night work and used the rest in rotation.

The rangy, long-legged Texas cattle, wild as they seemed on their home ranges, often became fairly tractable, good travelers on the trail, unless adverse circumstances turned them nervous or ornery. One of them always

turned out to be a natural leader, who took his position in the van of the column every morning and maintained it for the duration of the drive. If such an animal displayed particular aptitude for showing the way on the trail, a drover might use him over and over again for that purpose. Most of such natural leaders were steers, and of those that became well known as lead steers the most famous was Old Blue. It was said that Old Blue got to know the trail to Dodge City better than did most of the cowboys. Charlie Goodnight bought him from John Chisum in 1874, as part of a large herd. On the drive north, Blue, who was then a four-year-old, showed his prowess, taking his place at the lead each morning and staying there. At the end of the drive, instead of selling Blue with the rest of the herd, Goodnight kept him, and when the great cattleman began trailing stock regularly from his ranch in the Texas Panhandle to Dodge City, Old Blue was always in the lead. A brass bell was hung around his neck, and the rest of the cattle soon learned to follow its sound. For eight years Old Blue led the Goodnight herds on their northward treks, and in some of those years he made two trips. He never shied at sudden disturbances and disdained to take part in stampedes. The horns of Old Blue—he lived to be twenty—are on display in the Panhandle-Plains Historical Society in Canyon, Texas.

Others in the herd tended to maintain the same general position in the

Men like the range boss below, photographed in the early 1900's, were responsible for the welfare of valuable herds of cattle as they grazed on the open range. Important as the work of the range boss was, it was less demanding than the job of the trail boss, who guided the herds on the treacherous routes north in the days of the big trail drives.

trail column day after day. Habitual stragglers made up the tail end of the column, or the drag. Where practicable, the cattle were allowed to spread out in a loose, wide V for most of the day, and late in the afternoon were worked into a long column while they were eased toward the bedding ground, chosen by the trail boss who

had ridden on ahead during the day.

Two of the most experienced hands rode in the lead, or point, of the herd. These riders, sometimes called point men or point riders, directed the progress of the herd, holding it to the course indicated by the trail boss; guarded against mix-ups with other herds on the trail; and if trouble came,

tried to prevent stampedes from developing. Behind the point men, on each side of the herd and at spaced intervals, came swing riders, and following them were flank riders. Bringing up the rear were the drag riders. The drag riders had the least desirable of all jobs on the drive, "eating dust" and nursing along the stragglers.

For each of the first few days the cattle were urged along, perhaps to cover as much as 25 or 30 miles. With the home range once well behind them, the pace was eased to average about ten miles a day, more or less, depending on conditions of grass and water supply. The cowboys got the herd strung out and moving early in the morning, letting the cattle graze along for three or four miles in the desired direction, then driving them along steadily for a while. If possible, there was a halt for water about noon, after which the herd was again allowed to graze along until sundown approached. Sometime before dark the cowboys drove the herd onto the bedding ground, the cook having already set up camp nearby; here they rode around the herd in slowly contracting circles until, forced into a compact body, the cattle lay down. The horses were thrown into a rope corral or hobbled nearby; the tired men ate supper and rolled into their blankets—except those designated to guard the herd on the first night watch, which lasted until ten o'clock.

The men on night guard rode slowly around the bedded-down cattle. They might sing or hum or whistle a tune softly, especially if there were signs that the herd was getting restless.

The cowboys at left, gathered around their campfire, are making the vast darkness of a night on the trail more pleasant by telling jokes and tall tales. The man at far right who has just dismounted from his horse has come in from his turn at riding herd.

57

Oh say little dogies, when are
you goin' to lay down
And quit this forever shiftin' around?
My horse is leg-weary and
I'm awful tired,
But if you get away I'm sure
to get fired.

These ambling rhythms were the kind of lullabies that settled the herd. "One lazy old brindle steer," said cattleman John Young, "was particularly fond of 'One Evening in May' "— a waltz, played on the fiddle. Along about midnight there would be a general stir as the cattle heaved themselves to their feet, then lay down in another position. Watches changed on time told by the North Star, the last one going on duty from two o'clock until breakfast. Then came the catching-up and saddling of the horses, and the herd was lined out for another day on the trail.

The Texas longhorn herds marched northward, unguided by compass. If the streams they crossed flowed west to east, the trailsmen knew they were heading in the right direction. When they camped for the night, the wagon was drawn up with its tongue pointed at the North Star. When they started out again, at dawn, they were headed wagon tongue north.

A good trail boss conscientiously ranged far ahead of his herd every day to locate good bedding grounds and watering places and to lay out the route for the herd to follow. Many of the trails, especially in the earlier years, were not well defined, and some trail bosses favored cutoffs or special bypaths of their own making. There were, of course, only a limited number of good river crossings, so that trail herds tended to converge when ap-

proaching a large stream and diverge again after they were safely across. The point riders kept a sharp lookout for the far-off figure of the boss, who rode his horse back and forth in a pattern that signaled directions as to how he wanted the herd headed out. When a river was approached, he saw to it that the herd was well strung out and the leaders walking briskly. When the cattle waded in to drink, the pressure from those coming behind pushed them into deeper water and across to the far bank, the cowboys working hard to keep the column moving across and to prevent it from spreading out and bending downstream.

The trail boss had to be continuously alert to avoid conditions that might frighten the cattle and touch off a stampede. Longhorns shared the uneasiness that wilderness animals show around watering places, so a careful boss saw to it that ducks were shooed off the water before the herd arrived; a duck flying up while the cattle were drinking could trigger a wild run. For bedding grounds he chose the kind of level places that cattle would pick for themselves, not narrow valleys or rough-surfaced areas; he saw to it that they were well watered and full of grass before they lay down, and that the men's camp, not too far from the herd, was quiet and orderly.

Longhorns were, unfortunately, more liable to give way to the panic run of stampede than most other

The sad cowboys in this old photograph are standing at the graveside of a comrade who was killed when he fell beneath the hoofs of a stampeding herd. Despite the watchfulness of most cowboys for signs of a stampede, some men were killed by their own herds.

breeds of cattle. By their wild nature aware and sensitive to danger, they were always ready to raise their tails and head for the horizon. Then it might be "one jump to their feet and their second jump to hell," as an old-timer expressed it.

The worst stampedes were those that happened at night. The physical danger, considerable under any circumstances, was then enhanced by the darkness. Most trail drivers, however, seemed to worry more about cattle getting lost or injured, or the precious time it took to get the herd reassembled and under control again, than they did about the risks a stampede entailed for their own lives. Electrical storms, with thunder and lightning and sometimes pelting hailstones, probably caused more stampedes than anything else. Frank Dobie, in *A Vaquero of the*

of the circle climbing over each other. Constant flashes of lightning gave us glimpses of them. Balls of fire were playing on the tips of the long horns and the tips of our horses' ears . . . the wind was not yet blowing much, and the seething mass of cattle gave out waves of heat that were almost scorching."

Strange smells or sudden little noises could bring bedded cattle to their feet and set them off in a wild, earth-jarring run in the tick of a second. One time, a man helping a trail driver with a bunch of yearling longhorns being readied for the trail suddenly flashed a "bull's-eye" lantern from under his coat on a quiet, starlit night; the next minute, three hundred longhorns were on their feet and running—each one taking "a different course for the brush," as the man who recorded the incident said.

Other man-made hazards could send a whole herd into ground-shaking flight. Sometimes they were deliberate —Indians blanket-waving hundreds of cattle into stampeding so that they could get away with a few head; or cattle thieves scattering the Texans' trail herds and making off with as many head as they could before the animals could be rounded up again. At times they were accidental, as when

Brush Country, tells the story of a stampede triggered by lightning that John Young told him: "They started just as a flash of lightning made the whole world a blinding, blue white. It came from right over our heads and by the time the clap of thunder reached us the cattle were gone, the roar of their running mixed with the roar of the sky . . . the herd began to mill, running in a circle, the cattle in the center

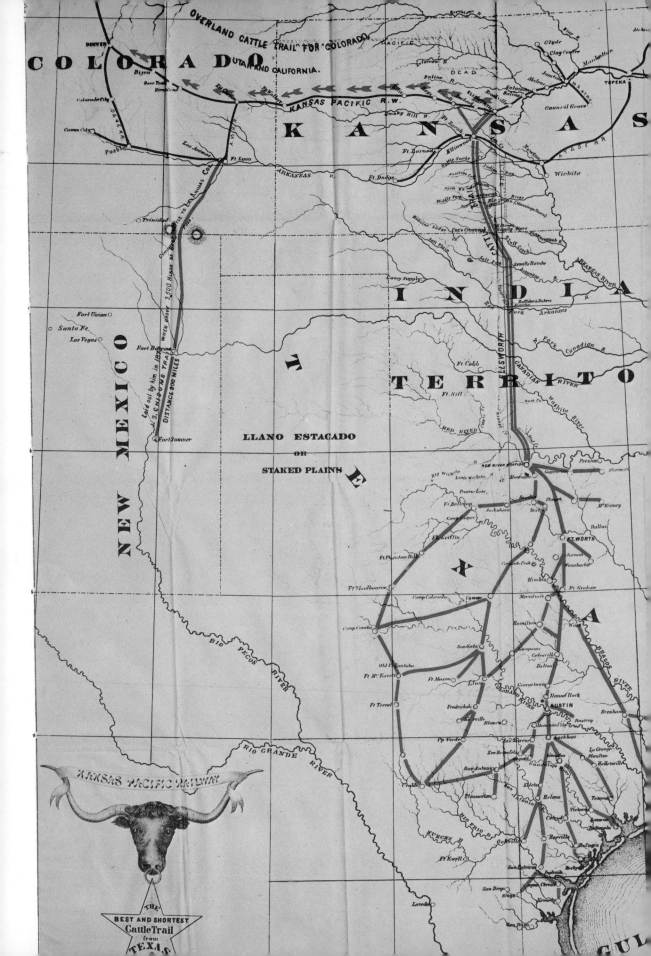

1,400 steers in a herd driven by John Barrows were being watered in the Yellowstone River after a long, dry march. They had just finished when from the cliffs across the river came the boom of dynamite blasts set off by Northern Pacific Railway construction workers. The steers ran two miles before the men could check them; and with the drive continuing along the river for several days after that, every time they put the cattle into the water they had to be ready to cope with a stampede as soon as the animals' thirst was quenched; it was a simple case of conditioned reaction.

David Shirk and George Miller drove a herd through from Texas to the Owyhee River in Idaho in April, 1871. The herd was made up of 1,500 head of four- and five-year-olds—one thousand to be Miller's, and 250 each going to David Shirk and a third partner, a man named Walters. One evening on the drive north, Miller and Shirk saw that there was a bad storm in the making, and prepared for a sleepless night. The herd was bedded down, quiet and content, when huge raindrops started falling and a great roar of wind signaled the storm's onset. Hailstorms came with the wind. The cattle got to their feet and started to drift. David was on his horse, trying to turn them back. The rest of the men were on the flanks, attempting to hold the herd together.

After an hour the torrential rain slackened and the flashes of lightning, which had been illuminating the night blackness, became less frequent. David and the other men had to rely on the sounds made by the cattle to tell where they were. Suddenly David's horse balked, refusing to go ahead, but instead of trusting the animal David dug in his spurs—and they plunged down a steep embankment, landing in water up to the stirrups. Afraid the cattle would come down on top of him, David started his horse through the water, which he realized was rising, toward the opposite shore—where he encountered a perpendicular bank higher than he could reach.

He rode and swam his horse downstream until he came to what seemed to be a small island. The level of the water was still rising rapidly, and David feared it would soon cover his bit of land. He called out, but could hear no answering hail. He felt for his matches and found them all soaked. Preferring the known risk to the unknown one, he decided to stay where he was.

He waited and waited, occasionally shouting at the top of his voice. At last he heard Miller calling, and at about the same time, he became aware that the water level was going down; his answering shout was one of double relief. The darkness began to abate as dawn showed gray in the east. After a while Miller appeared on the bank,

and David swam his horse to the shore and safety. He found that the others had managed to hold the herd together, but they were five miles from camp, soaking wet, chilled to the bone, and hungry. But David Shirk was alive, and glad of it.

While they were driving across Chickasaw territory, a band of Indians rode up and demanded payment for letting the white men pass through their land and use their grass. David knew that Miller, who was riding

The cowboy in the Frederic Remington painting at right is trying desperately to head off a stampede in his herd. The herd has been frightened by a raging storm with its loud thunder and sharp flashes of lightning.

somewhere ahead of the herd, had paid the toll while making a drive the year before, but he believed that no payment was necessary unless they made a permanent camp. He told this to the chief of the band.

The leader talked this over with his warriors, then answered the young white man. They wanted pay, he said, and if they did not get it they would fight. The Indians outnumbered the cowboys, fifteen to twelve, but David again showed that he did not bluff easily. He waved in the men, who had their rifles ready, and told the chief that they were ready to fight too. "I am not going to pay you one cent, or cattle either," he said.

The two groups faced each other for a tense minute before the chief turned his horse and led his followers away. When Miller returned and learned what had happened, he feared they were in for trouble; they doubled the guard that night, but the Indians did not come back. Later on, they learned

that the band of braves was on its way home from a buffalo hunt, and when they came across the trail herd "tried a round of blackmail," as David Shirk put it. It was customary, and many drovers preferred paying toll to courting trouble.

The unending grind of the trail went on, exhausting days and often sleepless nights, punctuated by mishaps. One day the cook drove his oxen-pulled wagon into a stream to cross it, without first giving them a chance to drink. The thirsty animals halted to dip their muzzles into the flowing water, and the wheels on one side of the stalled wagon settled into a quicksand bed. In another minute the wagon capsized, spilling provisions and cooking utensils into the water. The bedding floated

downstream but was recovered—thoroughly soaked.

A band of Indians stampeded their saddle band; fortunately, it was a moonlit night, and they were able to recover the horses at the end of a long chase. On one moonless night the cattle were stampeded by yelling, gunfiring raiders, whether Indians or whites the men did not know. More

than a hundred head were driven off, but when daylight came David, Miller, and Walters followed their trail and finally came within sight of them. The alarmed thieves shot several of the cattle, then fled. The three drovers did not try to give chase on their spent horses, but they recovered most of the stolen stock. For days afterward the herd was restless and jumpy, but handled with extra care and driven by easy stages, the cattle finally settled down. The trouble was past.

On October 12, they went into camp at the head of Bruneau Valley, where Miller and Walters were to remain. The drive had taken five months and seventeen days. On the fourteenth, David Shirk cut his share of the herd—224 head—out from the rest, becoming a small cattle owner on his own, and his own boss. He held them in winter quarters, letting them feed on white sage and bunch grass, and in the spring he sold them, including his calf crop. When he settled his share of the expenses of the drive, he found he had netted $2,160—no more than fair profit, considering the hard work, the danger, and his risk of losing everything.

Cattlemen were not the only Texans who ran into trouble with the Indians. On June 27, 1874, a party of about seven hundred Cheyenne, Comanche, and Kiowa Indians attacked a white buffalo hunters' camp (left) at Adobe Walls, Texas. The attack failed when the buffalo hunters were reinforced by other hunters who were in the vicinity.

Rustlers
and Barbed Wire

The greatest drives north from Texas took place in the summer of 1871. An estimated 700,000 cattle were driven to the Kansas plains to await buyers, but for half the cattle there was no market. The days passed into fall. The prairies around the cow towns were nearly grazed out by the waiting cattle. Snow fell early on the trail-gaunted herds, and the animals, used to a hot climate, did not know how to nuzzle through snow cover to the feed. One blizzard after another swept the plains that winter; day after day there was no letup to the furious snow-laden wind. Seventy-five per cent of the Texas cattle froze or starved during that awful winter. In the spring there were thousands of Texas hides to ship —and that was all.

Already there was a rival source for beef — sturdy crosses between longhorns and heavier Herefords and shorthorns ranging in the Dakotas and in Montana. In 1865, ranching had begun in the northern sector of the Great Plains.

The great herds of buffalo had always roamed there, feeding on the lush, foot-high bluestem (wheat grass) —grass tall enough to "roll in the wind like the sea," but the buffalo was hardy, covered with heavy hair against the incessant winter wind and snow. Before 1865 few men thought domestic ani-

Stocky English bulls like those on the opposite page were brought to America and crossed with the thinner Texas longhorn to produce better beef cattle. A Hereford is seen at top, and a shorthorn is shown at bottom.

mals could survive in what was called the Great American Desert. The area was described by Major Long, who led an expedition across it in 1819-20 as "almost wholly unfit for cultivation and of course uninhabitable by a people depending on agriculture . . ." For decades Major Long's map showing the Great American Desert was accepted as the standard map of the territory.

Then, in the fall of 1864, a drover called Newman was taking a supply train west to Fort Douglas in Utah and was caught by early snow on the Laramie Plains and forced to go into winter camp. Although he feared that the train's oxen would starve and be finished off by wolves if he turned them loose and let them fend for themselves, he had no alternative but to do so. Fortunately, the oxen chosen for supply trains were "tight and heavy made," and in the spring he found them still alive and in better condition than when they had been set loose. The velvety buffalo grass, which blanketed the plains all the way to the foothills of the Rockies, cured on the stem during the dry summers and retained all its food value as hay. Newman's oxen had thrived on it.

As soon as winter grazing on the northern plains was shown to be possible for domestic cattle, the industry started moving northward. Within fifteen years—from 1865 to 1880—cattle ranching spread out over the Great Plains. The Central Pacific and the Union Pacific railroads were joined,

The Crow Indians above, desperate for fresh meat, have shot a steer and are forced to

explain the shooting to the angry cowboys (right) from whose herd the animal strayed.

The Texas longhorn above, photographed in 1889, was a champion in European and American cattle contests. When he died he was thought to be at least twenty years old.

thereby crossing the plains, in 1869; the Great Northern Railroad was completed in 1893. This enabled cattlemen to ship their animals to the growing stockyards of Chicago. Also, the buffalo herds were being exterminated and the rich grassland that fed them was left for stockmen to use. Fantastic stories of easy money in cattle raising began to drift toward the East. Times were ripe for a new beef rush.

The Beef Bonanza; or How to Get Rich on the Plains, by James S. Brisbin, was the kind of book that fed the already excited public mind. "I believe that all the flocks and herds in the world could find ample pasturage on these unoccupied plains and the mountain slopes beyond," Brisbin wrote. He gave figures indicating that an investment of $100,000 could be doubled in five years, while at the same time paying a ten per cent dividend!

People who took part in the beef rush needed capital, which was not the case with those who went west to search for gold. The necessary investment was not large, however; and plenty of success stories were told, and believed, in which the main ingredient was luck. One such tale concerned a servant girl whose ranchman-employer owed her $150 in back pay and gave her fifteen cows to settle the debt, it being understood that the cattle and their increase were to stay on his range but bear her brand—and in ten years "she sold out to her master for $25,000." It was claimed that yearlings bought for five dollars a head could be fattened on free grass and sold for seventy dollars. According to one estimate, one hundred cows and their female descendants, kept for ten years, would grow into a herd of 1,428—and, besides, an equal number of bulls would have been produced, which could be sold!

With stories such as these circulating, it was small wonder that easterners as well as Englishmen, Scots, Canadians, and other foreigners came flocking to the Great Plains to become ranchers. These tenderfeet were often a source of amusement to the old-time cattlemen and their cowboys; but most of them had ready cash to invest, and the older ranges still had surplus cattle to sell them for stocking their new ranches. Midwestern farm cattle were being shipped to the new ranges. With so many eager newcomers adding to the demand, the prices for ordinary range stock began to climb; between 1879 and 1882 the price (by the herd) went from $7 or $8 to $12, then to $35 a head. Cattlemen could make a profit of 300 per cent on stock they had bought three years before.

So it was that by the summer of 1882 the great beef bonanza was on in full force. Men kept coming from everywhere to buy herds of cattle and "range rights" (the exclusive use, for herding and grazing purposes, of land that belonged to the public).

One of the greenhorn easterners who established himself as a cattle rancher was a young New Yorker named Theodore Roosevelt. He came west originally to hunt buffalo, took an immediate and strong liking to the country, and in 1883 bought four hundred head of cattle bearing the Maltese Cross brand that were being run on a range near the Little Missouri River in western North Dakota. A year later Roosevelt added one thousand head of cattle to his herd. He also acquired a second place, which he called his Elkhorn Ranch and where he set up headquarters; cattle on this ranch were branded on one side with an elk horn, in outline, and on the other side with a triangle.

Lincoln Lang, who was one of Roosevelt's Badlands neighbors, was impressed with the way T.R. held his own on the district roundup, asking for and receiving no favors, "riding circle twice a day, often taking the outer swing, taking his turn on day-herd or night-guard duty, helping with the cutting out operations, branding calves, and so on; he was in the saddle all of 18 hours per day . . . frequently riding over a hundred miles within the 24 hours." He recalled how T.R. rode a bad horse one day; when he mounted, the animal pitched and bucked viciously, but the young New Yorker stayed on, even though he "pulled leather" (gripped the saddle horn with one hand, roll-cantle with the other). There was a stigma attached to doing so, as Lang noted, but a still worse one to getting thrown. Roosevelt hung on to the end, even though he lost his hat, his eyeglasses, and his six-shooter.

Another colorful character of the time and place was a Frenchman, the Marquis de Mores, who in 1883 founded a town where the Northern Pacific Railroad crossed the Little Missouri. He named it Medora, after his American wife. De Mores invested several hundred thousand dollars in a meat-packing plant at Medora, and in several other ambitious schemes, but in 1887 he gave it all up and returned to France with his beautiful wife. Before he left he had become involved in a dispute over fences that led to a fatal shooting (for which he was tried and found not guilty); and he and Roosevelt once had a disagreement so violent that the handsome marquis was alleged to have challenged Roosevelt to a gun duel.

The grass was "free" in vast portions of the plains and prairies. It grew on land that belonged to the public, title being vested in either the states or the federal government. Men who owned great herds that grazed over millions of acres had no right to those acres—except whatever right lay in the fact that they got there first. Range outfits that ran tens of thousands of cattle

These settlers (seen in part of a poster illustration used by Buffalo Bill to advertise his Wild West Show) are fleeing from a prairie fire. Such fires, which could be equally destructive to cattle and to men, were sometimes set by the Indians in hopes of frightening away the unwanted white men.

often did not own a single square foot of the land used for grazing, and sometimes not even the land where their ranch buildings stood.

A stockman could acquire control of range rights by placing a notice in a a newspaper listing his brand and fixing the extent of the range he claimed by naming boundary creeks and other landmarks. His claim would be similarly recorded, with his brand, in state or territory brand books. Afterward, he maintained control of his claim under a "customary range" law, which provided for fines and jail sentences for anyone who drove stock off their customary range without the owner's permission. If courts had trouble—and they often did—in deciding what was customary range for stock that often wandered afar, many ranchers did not hesitate to take direct action and do some law enforcing of their own.

Another method of maintaining range control was the roundup boycott. When their customary range was

invaded by late arrivals who shoved new herds into the region, the established cattlemen refused to work the invaders' cattle—meaning that the newcomers would not be permitted to take part in the common roundup. Thus, in 1885, when an outsider brought a herd onto range already claimed by another outfit, the local cattlemen's association condemned his action and voted not to handle his cattle in the district roundup. The newcomer surrendered to the pressure and took his herd somewhere else. Later on, other late-comers on the range fought the earlier claimants by banding together and conducting roundups of their own ahead of the common district roundups. This gave the "sooners," as they came to be called, an opportunity to brand all the mavericks for themselves, a chance that most

of them did not hesitate to put to profitable use. Sometimes they also ran the older ranchers' stock hard so that they lost flesh and had their market value decreased. All the advantages did not lie with the established range claimants.

These "grass pirates," as they were called by ranchers with prior claims, were sometimes small operators who were out to build up herds by the simple method of putting their own brands on all the unbranded animals they found and could rope on unfenced range. It was not an unusual practice in open-range days, when mixed herds grazed over one region. Nor was it easy to prove wrongful intent, as it was perfectly possible to misbrand an animal by accident. So the "sooners" were under constant temptation to skim the cream off the open range.

More serious than the branding of mavericks or calves by some of the smaller stockmen were the raids of bands of thieves who stole both cattle and horses. As time went on, their operations grew bolder and more widespread, although many cattlemen's associations hired stock detectives to combat the rustlers. Conditions worsened to the point where horses were being stolen from unguarded stables as well as from pastures. At the end of the 1883 fall roundup, some ranchers found they had lost three per cent or more of their cattle to rustlers, and stern action was demanded. Montana ranchers met and formed a Montana stockgrowers' association. A general meeting was held in Miles City in April, 1884; representatives trom western North Dakota attended also, including Theodore Roosevelt and the Marquis de Mores.

It was a stormy meeting. Many of the ranchers there demanded that an army of cowboys be organized to raid the hideouts of the rustler gangs. Granville Stuart, president of the association, spoke against it, much to the disgust of the fiery Frenchman, who accused Stuart of "backing water." Roosevelt sided with De Mores; but Stuart was upheld when a majority of the members voted to take no action against the rustlers. This information was allowed to reach the outlaws, who happily made preparations for what they now thought would be a prosperous year for them.

Actually, Granville Stuart and the others had put over an elaborate deception. Following the spring roundup, secret meetings were held at the ranches of Stuart and some of the other big cattle raisers. Stock detectives reported on the operations of the rustlers, upon whom they had been spying, and plans were made to strike, under Stuart's directions. In July, 1884, a small force of riders started raiding one outlaw stronghold after another. Some sixty rustlers were shot or hanged. Charges were made later that the Stranglers, as the self-appointed law enforcers were called by their critics, roughed up a number of innocent men and tried to drive some of

Chicago's Union Stockyards in 1866 (above), a livestock market, followed the costly practice of shipping live animals to meat dealers for slaughter. Gustavus Swift (left) changed this in 1875, when he transferred his business to Chicago and began slaughtering animals on the spot and then shipping the meat. The poster below was issued by a meat packer.

The cow towns of the West were full of quick money and bored cowboys who were fast with a gun. The cowboy in the painting above by Frederic Remington, called An Argument with the Town Marshal, *is about to settle his dispute with the law by shooting it out. His battleground is a typical western main street.*

The men in the picture below have taken the law into their own hands and are performing an execution without benefit of a trial or a jury verdict. The victim's offense was probably horse theft, a grave crime in a world where horses were necessary for making a living as well as for transportation.

The grim westerners above are coming from a "necktie party"—they have hanged a man from the tree in the background. In the early days of the western cow towns, before recognized law enforcement officers had taken over, crimes were punished by groups of citizens. Men like the dashing stagecoach robber at right were a menace in the early West, for they took advantage of the lack of law enforcement and seized money being carried over the lonely trails.

79

the small ranchers out of the country.

Stuart personally led the raid on a gang that hung out along the Missouri River near Cow Island. Their leader was John Stringer—called Stringer Jack—a former buffalo hunter who had turned cattle rustler and horse thief. At the end of a long fight, during which the outlaws' cabin was burned down by the vigilantes, with some of the men still inside it, all but five of the gang were dead—shot or burned to death. Four of the five who escaped were captured later by United States soldiers and turned over to a federal marshal; but a posse of the Stranglers took the prisoners away from the marshal and hanged them.

Once the organized gangs had been wiped out, the association ranchers never let the problem get out of control again. Of the cowboys who dared to use a long rope and a running iron, some got their herds started and then turned honest. Less fortunate ones served prison terms. And a few—those who were caught in the act by ranchers who preferred gun law to legal justice —had their careers, and their lives, ended on the spot.

The losses inflicted on the cowmen by range thieves, however, were dwarfed by those visited on them by the workings of nature. By 1884, the western ranges were seriously overstocked. The natural grasses had been thinned by the grazing of vast herds, until it took about ten acres of ordinary range to support one cow. Many ranchers were trying to get by with five or six acres per cow. In two years, from 1882 to 1884, the seemingly endless rich grass of the plains had been grazed down to a danger point. Wiser cattlemen shook their heads in apprehension.

After passage of the Federal Homestead Law, people had come into the public lands of the West, each one claiming his quarter-section (160 acres), starting a farm, enclosing pastures, and fencing in water holes. Sheepmen brought in their herds, and the sharp hoofs of the "woolies" often destroyed the roots of the grasses that the sheep grazed so close to the soil. The use of barbed wire, introduced in 1874, spread rapidly, converting what had been a few big pastures into many small ones. At first, its growing use led to fierce disputes and fence-cutting fights so serious that one rancher said he wished the inventor of barbed wire "had it all wound around him in a ball and the ball rolled into hell." By 1880, however, a great many cattle pastures were enclosed by the twisted barbed strands.

The days of the open range were already numbered, then, when the elements struck a series of final, decisive blows. First came a serious drought, worse in Texas than elsewhere, but affecting most of the western ranges to some degree. Cattle prices began to go down. Then came the severe winter of 1884-85. A raging blizzard late in December laid a thick coat of ice and sleet over the grass. Cattle drifted south from the northern ranges, their

Winter was a bitter season for the cowboy and his horse (above) on the open range. The cowboy's life depended on chopping wood and keeping his fire going. Even the horses were chilled despite their shaggy winter coats.

The hungry cowboys below are eating in back of the chuck wagon, on the range. The food and cooking utensils were kept in the wagon; the cook, always popular with the hands, prepared the meals over a campfire.

tails to the howling winds from the Arctic. There were still few fences in the north to stop them and they continued on and on until they reached the giant, 170-mile-long drift fence that stockmen had built in the neutral strip. There many of them piled up and froze to death. Most of those that got past that barrier—using mounds of dead bodies as ramps, or managing to break the wire—met their fate at a second great fence farther south.

In the spring of 1885 Texas cowboys found carcasses, and some live, skeleton-thin cattle, bearing brands from ranges five hundred miles away. Tens of thousands of frozen corpses were thawing out along the lines of the fences. Ranches in northern Oklahoma had lost fifty per cent or more of their stock. After months of hunting, one outfit had found only 2,500 head of the 20,000 they had before. In Nebraska, the huge Bay State Cattle Company lost 100,000 head. Ten miles of the creek bed on its range was choked with dead animals, and the company was ruined.

The cattlemen had suffered a terrible blow, but more was to follow.

Huge roundups were held in Texas to collect and drive back the storm-lost cattle that were overcrowding ranges sparsely grassed from 1884's low rainfall; and 1885 was another drought year. The burning dryness spread from Texas ranges into Kansas, into Nebraska, into Wyoming and Montana. Hardhit by the heavy winter-kill and now besieged by the widening drought, ranchers rushed cattle to market and had to sell them at ruinously low prices.

Again in the spring of 1886 the rainfall was below average. Springs and creeks and water holes were drying up. Big prairie fires took their toll of what grass was left. Then came the fall, and old-timers began to notice ominous signs. Prairie dogs holed up early. Animals' coats seemed heavier than usual. Birds started their migrations earlier than they ordinarily did. Elk joined the march south. Granville Stuart saw arctic owls, something new to Montana's Judith Basin.

The early snow was welcomed at first, since it was believed that the drought was ended. But the top layer melted a little and then froze, covering the grass so the stock could not get to

The cold and snow of winter presented many problems, both on the trail and on the range. The cowboy in the photograph above is rescuing a calf who strayed from the herd during a blinding snowstorm. The lone trail driver in the photograph below watches as his herd moves through the snow. He cannot let them stop or slow down because of the cold.

OVERLEAF: When the cowboy went into desert areas, the water hole became the most important thing in his life—for it often meant life or death. The cowboys in this Frederic Remington painting are defending the water hole from another party.

83

All sorts of people came West during the beef bonanza to become ranchers. The Marquis de Mores (left) and his wife (above) were two of the most colorful of the ranchers.

Theodore Roosevelt (right), who would one day be President of the United States, became a rancher in North Dakota during the boom and was a neighbor of the Marquis de Mores. One of the brands used by Roosevelt is shown above.

it. There were two blizzards in December; and then on January 9, after a long clear spell, the cold wind howled from the north, snow began to fall, and the temperature dipped far below zero. The great storm lasted ten days without any letup. All that the cattle had to eat was the sagebrush tips that showed above the snow and the bark on willows and low tree branches. They gathered around ranch houses, bawling piteously; but except for a few small ranchers who had grown hay for fenced-in herds, their owners could do nothing. Starving cattle wandered into towns and ate the tar paper off the outer walls of shacks.

It was the knockout blow. The spring roundup of 1887 was the grimmest, saddest one in range history. A loss of 90 per cent was not uncommon. Carcasses choked dry stream beds and dammed up creeks. Buzzards blackened the skies. Wolves and coyotes, the only four-legged life that prospered through that winter, were gorged, fat, and lazy. A sickening stench hovered over the sad prairie earth.

Even Granville Stuart, the acknowledged leader of Montana's cowmen, whose DHS riders had worked hard and ceaselessly to bring the big ranch's seasoned herd through the winter, suffered stunning losses. His cattle had drifted so badly that it was a year before some of the survivors were found; he finally figured he had lost 66 per cent of his stock. No one had been spared. Throughout Montana, some $20,000,000 worth of cattle were gone.

When the dazed ranchers realized the extent of the damage, many of them took their losses and quit. A few of the owners, men of great faith and determination, tightened their belts and made new starts. Here and there a cowboy who had frugally saved up his wages bought remnants of herds from ranchers who were on their way out of the business and out of the country for good, and started a brand of his own; but all that most ranch hands got out of the long winter was the memory of riding all day without any dinner in savage sub-zero cold, doing their best to save the walking bags of bones that were the boss's cattle.

The great beef bonanza passed into history during the winter of 1886-87. The day of the longhorn was past. Cattle, the stockmen saw now, had to be cared for and fed to get them through the winters. Such care and expense would be wasted on the long-legged, lean-flanked stock from the south. High-priced bulls would have to be brought in to breed-up the herds and produce heavier-meated animals. More pastures had to be fenced off, so more barbed wire had to be ordered. Shorter-legged stock could not be expected to walk miles for water, so wells and stock water ponds had to be dug and windmills erected.

Cowboys who considered post-hole digging and hay-pitching beneath them would have to saddle up and ride for new frontiers. The future looked gloomy for the knights of the range.

The
Range Wars

Quarrels in the cow towns of the West were often settled in a sudden burst of gun-
fire, as in the painting below. The playing cards scattered about on the ground indicate
that the man who has been shot may have been guilty of that grave sin—cheating.

On the western frontier, courts of law were few and far between, and men could not count on them to settle disputes. Besides, the judges who presided over them often found it difficult to apply to the conditions of the frontier laws that had been made to fit the needs of settled communities in the East. Vast distances lay between the towns, and it was easy for a man who

was wanted by the law to lose himself in the emptiness of the plains. With judges and police officers hard to find, law-abiding men needed to have courage, determination, and skill with firearms. The West often seemed lawless, and westerners often seemed to be persistent lawbreakers. In fact, the West was slowly developing a set of rules that would fit the conditions of life on a new frontier.

Gun fights were common in the rough cattle-shipping towns and boom towns, but these personal duels were not historically significant. There were other conflicts, involving large numbers of men, which were widespread enough to be termed "range wars."

In one of these—more widely known than most because the almost legendary Billy the Kid took part in it—New Mexico's Lincoln County War, a dozen or more men met their deaths. Several of the territory's most powerful and important men became involved in it. The struggle was waged over range rights and cattle markets, business interests in the town of Lincoln, and political control of the county.

On one side were L. G. Murphy, who owned a ranch as well as a large store, a hotel, and a saloon in Lincoln; his business partners, James Dolan and John Riley; and William Brady, the county sheriff. Arrayed against them were John "Jinglebob" Chisum, who owned a huge ranch on the Pecos River; John Tunstall, an Englishman on whose Rio Feliz ranch William Bonney (Billy the Kid) worked briefly

William Bonney, better known as Billy the Kid, posed for the photograph above toward the end of his short life; he was shot at the age of twenty-one. Billy, as seen here, bears little resemblance to the romantic hero that legend has made of him. The poster on the opposite page is probably not the genuine poster which offered a reward for Billy's capture; a mistake has been made as to his last name, and there is no record of a sheriff named Jim Dalton. The announcement may well have been just an advertising stunt.

as a wrangler; and Alexander Mc-Sween, a lawyer who, using capital furnished by Tunstall and Chisum, established a mercantile and banking business in Lincoln to compete with Murphy, Dolan, and Riley.

The new place threatened to undercut the business and the profits of the older firm. Alarmed, Murphy, Dolan, and Riley sought ways and means to eliminate their competitors. To satisfy certain legal claims filed against McSween, Sheriff Brady and his deputies took over property in the McSween-Tunstall store. Then a sheriff's posse rode to Tunstall's ranch with instructions to take over his cattle and horses; it was claimed that as Tunstall's partner McSween owned them too. There were several men with criminal records in the large force under deputized Billy Morton, a fact of which Sheriff Brady was apparently unaware. In an encounter on the road from Lincoln, Tunstall was shot and killed. Posse members claimed he had shot first, but some of his men who had been nearby asserted that the Englishman was shot in cold blood.

It was the beginning of a savage conflict that went on for months. Billy the Kid, who readily enlisted in the fight, was supposed to have felt strong ties of loyalty to Tunstall, who was a friendly, warmhearted man. Three weeks after the Englishman's death, a number of men were deputized by a justice of the peace who issued warrants for the arrest of some of the members of the group that had killed Tunstall. This posse was headed by Dick Brewer, a neighbor of the slain man who had worked for him as foreman. Billy the Kid rode with them, although he was not a deputy. They captured two of the men charged with the killing, Frank Baker and Billy Morton, and held them overnight. The next day they started out for Chisum's ranch, near Lincoln, with the prisoners, but on the way Baker and Morton were shot and killed, and so was a member of the posse who was suspected of being a friend of Morton's. Who fired the fatal shots was never established, although Baker and Morton are usually included in the mythical list of twenty-one victims credited to Billy the Kid. Of course, it was claimed that the men were shot while trying to escape.

Coming to Lincoln to investigate conditions, the governor of New Mexico stripped the authority from the justice of the peace who had deputized Brewer and his men. After ruling that law enforcement in the county was solely in the hands of Sheriff Brady and Judge Bristol, the governor left. Not long after that, Sheriff Brady and Deputy Sheriff Hindman were shot down as they walked along a street in Lincoln. The killers were concealed behind a high gate or a wall near the Tunstall store, but witnesses identified them as Billy the Kid, Hendry Brown, and John Middleton.

Three days later, "Buckshot" Roberts, who may have been a member of the posse that killed Tunstall, was attacked by a band of McSween-Tunstall

men led by Dick Brewer. Roberts was killed, but only after he had downed Brewer and wounded a couple of the others. Billy the Kid was in this fight, too, but the bullet that ended Robert's life was fired by Charlie Bowdre, a close pal of the Kid's.

There followed weeks of turmoil and violence. The battle lines were drawn, and people who did not want to take sides left the county. Men rode toward Lincoln, singly or in small groups, planning to join in the promised hostilities or to observe the final showdown.

On July 14, McSween arrived with his party and quartered about twelve men in his house. The rest went to the houses of his allies or scattered to

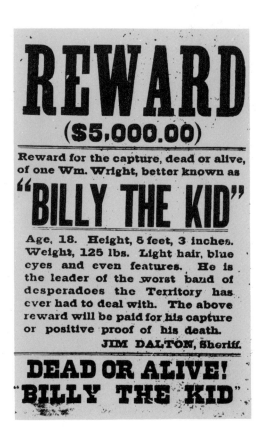

REWARD

($5,000.00)

Reward for the capture, dead or alive, of one Wm. Wright, better known as

"BILLY THE KID"

Age, 18. Height, 5 feet, 3 inches. Weight, 125 lbs. Light hair, blue eyes and even features. He is the leader of the worst band of desperadoes the Territory has ever had to deal with. The above reward will be paid for his capture or positive proof of his death.

JIM DALTON, Sheriff.

DEAD OR ALIVE!
"BILLY THE KID"

the town's outskirts. The sheriff's men hung around the court house and the Murphy store. For three days there were sporadic exchanges of gunfire, and Lincoln residents ventured on the streets at the risk of being hit by a stray bullet. Little business could be done with the opposing forces trading shots, mostly at long distance. The few casualties were minor, and then one of the men holed up in McSween's house took a pot shot at a soldier on leave from nearby Fort Stanton.

That incident brought the fort's commander riding into town at the head of a large force of United States troops. Warrants were issued against McSween and others for assault with intent to kill. With the army standing by, some of the sheriff's men managed to set McSween's house afire, the besieged occupants having refused to surrender. Not until the flames drove them out did the men inside dash from the building. It was now dark, but in the flickering light of the burning house the fleeing figures were perfect targets for the besieging gunmen. Mc-Sween and three of his men were killed. A rancher named Beckwith was the only fatality on the sheriff's side. Billy the Kid managed to escape, and

so did the rest of the McSween men.

The power of the McSween faction was now broken, and Chisum did nothing to rally the group. The men dispersed and organized resistance to the Dolan-Riley group, and the sheriff's office came to an end, but the county was in a state of uncertainty for months. Rustlers and horse thieves took advantage of the unsettled conditions, and range crime flourished. Lew Wallace, former Union Army general, now best known as the author of *Ben Hur*, was appointed governor of the territory and by vigorous action made some progress in pacifying Lincoln County. In November, 1878, he issued a general pardon for all offenses committed in the county during the "war," to remain in effect as long as those concerned kept the peace and conducted themselves as good citizens.

On February 18, 1879, however, Huston Chapman, who had been a strong supporter of McSween during the hostilities and who had been heaping accusations and scorn on his enemies since McSween's death, was shot and killed in Lincoln. Two mem-

The saloon was the place where a cowboy could find amusement, companionship, and respite from the hardships of the trail and the loneliness of the range. Below, a few high-spirited boys whoop it up after visiting town.

bers of the Murphy-Dolan group named Campbell and Evans were accused of the crime, and Governor Wallace ordered them arrested. Learning that Billy the Kid had been at the scene of the shooting, Wallace promised the young outlaw immunity if he would testify as to what he knew about the murder of Chapman and also about the cattle rustling that had been stripping the ranges along the Pecos. In a secret meeting, the Kid agreed to do so; but the story got out, and Campbell and Evans broke jail and fled. However, the Kid, keeping his promise, submitted to arrest and gave his testimony before a grand jury.

Two hundred indictments were issued, most of them naming men who had fought on the sheriff's side in the struggle, but in nearly all cases the accused men came under the terms of the governor's amnesty and were never tried. The district attorney refused to free the Kid, on the grounds that he had not been conducting himself as a "good citizen" since the time of the governor's action. However, he contrived to escape from jail and again was on the loose.

Following his testimony in the grand jury hearings and his escape from jail, the Kid and several other hard characters plunged into a career of cattle rustling and horse stealing, gambling, and carousing. There was a legend that the Kid led a gang of forty or fifty men, but actually the group never numbered more than eight or ten.

In January, 1880, he killed a man in a saloon brawl. Later that year he and two of his men were involved in the murder of a deputy sheriff. He had been stealing cattle in the Texas Panhandle and selling them in New Mexico. The aroused Panhandle ranchers organized an association and sent representatives to New Mexico to recover their cows and help the local officers wipe out the band of thieves. The governor proclaimed a reward of $500 for "the delivery of Bonney, alias 'the Kid' to the Lincoln County sheriff." An organized posse took the trail of the gang. In December, Tom O'Folliard, one of the Kid's men, was killed in an ambush staged by Pat Garrett, then the sheriff of Lincoln County. Four days after that Garrett and his posse killed Charlie Bowdre and captured the Kid and three others at their cabin hide-out.

Imprisoned in Santa Fe, the Kid wrote four notes to Governor Wallace, pleading for an interview. He was unsuccessful. Brought to trial, he was found guilty of the murder of Sheriff Brady and was sentenced to hang. Taken to Lincoln to be executed, he escaped from jail after shooting two guards to death, rode east to the Pecos River country, and "went on the dodge." Someone tipped off Sheriff Garrett that the Kid was hanging around Fort Sumner, so Garrett went there with two deputies. The evening he arrived, he was sitting in the dark in Pete Maxwell's house, talking to Maxwell. The Kid, unaware that Garrett was there, walked into the house

Governor Lew Wallace of New Mexico (above) and Pat Garrett (left), sheriff of Lincoln County, New Mexico, were two of the last men with whom Billy the Kid tangled. It was Wallace who refused to help Billy out of his difficulties in Santa Fe, and Pat Garrett who finally shot Billy in Pete Maxwell's house (below) in Fort Sumner, New Mexico.

In the days of the beef bonanza and the range wars, the Texas plains (right) at times resembled battlefields. This grim scene, painted by Frederic Remington, shows what could happen when armed cowboys from rival ranches fought over ownership of unbranded cattle.

—he was on good terms with Maxwell— and entered the room where the two men were. Seeing another figure beside Maxwell, he whispered, *"Quién es?"* (Who is it?). They were the Kid's last words. Garrett, who had his gun drawn, fired twice; and Henry McCarty, alias William H. Bonney, alias Billy the Kid, was dead.

It was an unromantic ending but a fitting one. Billy the Kid had taken the lives of half a dozen men (perhaps as many as nine, although this figure is difficult to prove). Pat Garrett, who claimed that the Kid died with a gun in his hand, was certainly justified in shooting without giving prior warning. It was not a duel under a code of honor; Garrett was acting as an officer of the law against a known outlaw, a killer.

A better example of a range war— because struggle for control of the range was not complicated by other factors—is the Johnson County War of 1892. Most of the Wyoming range lands were under the domination of powerful ranchers who had driven great herds in from the south soon after the Civil War and of large land and cattle companies owned by outside investors, many of them British.

By the 1880's newcomers were arriving in the territory, homesteading claims, starting farms and small ranches. The big operators looked on them as nuisances; the latecomers resented the wealth and power of the cattle barons; antagonism built up, and soon gunmen were hired to patrol the ranges of the big outfits. The newcomers retaliated by slipping their brands on some of the ranchers' calves, and when they wanted fresh beef to eat they slaughtered a steer belonging to a big outfit and buried the hide. Taking advantage of the ill feeling, rustlers took their toll of the herds, knowing that the victims would blame someone on the other side. The Wyoming Stock Growers Association, dom-

inated by the big ranchers, did what it could, but more and more the range was being cut up into small holdings, more little people kept flocking in, electing sheriffs and brand inspectors favorable to them, and packing juries that set free men accused of rustling or brand-changing.

With the power of the big ranchers being challenged ever more seriously, direct and ruthless action was taken. A man named Jim Averill and a woman known as "Cattle Kate," suspected of stealing stock, were brutally lynched and hanged. A horse rancher accused of range theft was taken from his home and hanged. Opposition to the big ranchers kept on growing as local officials and newspapers began to stand up for the rights of homesteaders and small ranchers.

Finally, the large ranch owners planned a secret campaign to make an example of Johnson County, where the power of the newcomers was most pronounced. Men like Tom Horn—a range detective who liked to boast about the men he had killed—were sent far and wide to recruit an army of gun fighters. A special train brought twenty-five hard-eyed Texans to Cheyenne, where they were joined by members of the Wyoming Regulators, a vigilante organization that included ranch owners, foremen and managers, and range detectives. The train took them all on to Casper, where they saddled horses and rode north toward Buffalo, the county seat of Johnson County. Their leader was carrying a "dead list"—the names of seventy men marked for assassination, including that of Red Angus, the county sheriff. They were seen leaving the train at Casper, and word of their coming traveled ahead of them.

Instead of hurrying on to strike hard and swiftly at Buffalo, the invaders turned off their course to attack an isolated cabin. Word had reached them that Nate Champion, a man whose name was high on the dead list, was there. A Texan, Champion was a former top-hand cowboy who now ran a few cattle of his own, defying the big operators, who accused him of being a ringleader of the rustlers. They expected their grim business with Champion would take an hour or so, after which they would ride on to Buffalo.

Surrounding the cabin before daybreak, the vigilantes picked off Champion's partner, Nick Ray, when he stepped out the door. Champion himself then jumped out, gun in one hand, and under intense fire helped Ray back into the cabin, wounding one of the attackers with a pistol shot while doing so. This happened early in the morning. During the remainder of the day, Champion held off the half-a-hundred men who kept the cabin under siege

by rushing back and forth, shooting first from one side, then another. Living up to his reputation as a crack shot, he wounded two more of the invaders. While keeping them at bay, he tended his mortally wounded friend and every now and then found time to jot down a few lines in a little notebook, leaving a record of that dreadful day.

"It is now about two hours since the first shot," he wrote. "Nick is still alive. . . . Boys, there is bullets coming in like hail. Them fellows is in such shape I can't get at them. They are shooting from the stable and river and back of the house."

Meanwhile the gun fighters were arguing among themselves. The attack on Buffalo, where they expected to find a good many men on the dead list, was supposed to start that night. But they would not chance rushing the cabin, and no matter how much lead they poured into it the amazing Champion kept returning their fire.

During a lull, some time after Nick Ray had breathed his last, Nate Champion wrote a few more lines:

"Boys, I feel pretty lonesome just now. I wish there was someone here

The Johnson County War of 1892, fought in Johnson County, Wyoming, was a bitter conflict between the big cattlemen and small ranchers who settled in cabins like the one on the opposite page. William Angus, called "Red," was the sheriff of Johnson County who tried to defend the small ranchers. Added trouble in Wyoming was caused by gangs of rustlers like the Wild Bunch, and by ranchers who bought rustled cattle, like "Cattle Kate" and her gentleman friend James Averill.

William Angus

James Averill

A cabin at
Hole-in-the-Wall,
Wyoming

Ella Watson ("Cattle Kate")

The Wild Bunch

The poster at left, issued in 1874, told the farmers of America about an amazing new invention just patented by Joseph Glidden—barbed wire. The manufacturers' claims for their new product did not prove to be exaggerated, for barbed wire indeed changed the history of the West; it also changed the course of the American cattle industry. This poster was the first printed to advertise barbed wire. It was issued in Illinois, where cattlemen sold their stock at market.

The cabin and corral in the painting at right belonged to a nester, one of the group of small ranchers who attempted to make a place for themselves in range country that had originally been the private preserve of the big cattlemen. The range wars started, in part, because of the nesters' arrival.

with me so we could watch all sides at once. They may fool around until I get a good shot before they leave."

In the afternoon, Jack Flagg, another man on the dead list, approached Champion's cabin during a quiet interval, unaware that anything was wrong. He was recognized and the gunmen shot at him, but by bending low and spurring hard he got away.

The invaders were desperate. They knew Flagg would spread the alarm, and there was no telling how many men might gather to ride against them. They piled brush and planks on a wagon, set fire to it, and pushed it against the cabin. Inside, Champion was wounded, and his ammunition was running low. He watched the flames spread and the room fill with smoke, then covered his partner's body with a blanket and made his final entry in the notebook:

"The house is all fired. Good-by, boys, if I never see you again. Nathan D. Champion."

He put the notebook in his pocket and, holding his rifle, jumped out of a window and dashed for cover. At first drifting smoke hid him, but then he was spotted and a score of rifles cracked. He fired one shot before he went down and lay still. Someone pinned a note on his shirt: "Cattle Thieves Beware." The name of Nate Champion was crossed off the dead list. The blood-smeared notebook was found in his pocket.

Although it was nearing nightfall, the vigilantes started for Buffalo. A dozen miles from town they were met by a man who waved them back frantically. He had been spying for them in Buffalo, and he warned that a hundred local men were headed their way, with more gathering in the town. The

invaders retreated to the TA ranch house where they were now besieged by superior forces. The embattled Johnson County men were getting ready to push a wagon loaded with dynamite into the TA building when the Texans and Regulators were saved by the timely arrival of United States troops from Fort McKinney.

So the Johnson County War was over—ingloriously, for the invaders—almost before it had begun. One courageous fighting man — who might or might not have been a rustler, as charged—had thwarted the ambitious schemes of the big ranch owners. The invaders were taken back to Cheyenne under army escort, to protect them from indignant county residents. The "war" had settled nothing; rustling went on and the settlers kept coming into the area.

Another source of trouble on the range was the use of barbed wire for fences. It was much more effective than plain wire, and its use was doubly resented by those who, for any reason, wanted to keep the range open. At first the big ranchers fought it when homesteaders used it to fence off water; later, they decided it was cheaper to string barbed wire than it was to hire cowhands to ride boundary lines. Huge tracts of public land were fenced by ranchers who had no right to do so; eventually they were forced to remove it or to buy up the land they had enclosed. Some diehards attacked the new fences with wire cutters; in Texas, it led to hostilities serious enough to be called the Fence Cutter War—but barbed wire had come to stay. Eventually, laws were passed that made fence cutting a major crime. By the mid-1880's Texas Rangers were enforcing the requirement that a gate must be set in every three miles of fence. Huge ranches like the XIT of Texas were completely enclosed with barbed wire; and barbed wire also provided the cheap fencing that enabled homesteaders to protect their fields from the cowmen's grazing herds.

Gradually, the laws concerning grass and water rights were developed to fit the conditions of the prairies and the arid regions, so there were fewer reasons for open conflict. The wild Indians of the West had been tamed. Now it was the white man's turn to surrender some of his freedom of action as the frontier regions became more settled.

The photograph below shows the dried carcass of a cow hanging on a barbed wire fence. The cattle of the West had as hard a time as the ranchers getting used to the new fences.

After years of fighting barbed wire, the big cattlemen discovered that it was less expensive to use it than to hire cowboys to ride herd on their animals. Sheep ranchers such as the man at right, shown with his flock and dogs, used it extensively to protect their herds. The result was that homesteaders, arriving in what they thought were public lands, often found them cut up by fences. To combat the ranchers they took the law into their own hands (below) and cut the barbed wire. The men are masked to prevent them from being recognized.

The Cowboys

In the painting below, cowboys are performing one of their rougher and more exciting jobs—"breaking" horses (getting them accustomed to saddles, bridles, and riders). A large ranch with many cowboys on its payroll could afford to send a whole group of men onto the range to set up a breaking camp. Here they would catch and corral the horses they wanted for use on the ranch and those they wanted to sell, and break them.

Your grub is bread and bacon
And coffee black as ink;
The water is so full of alkali
It is hardly fit to drink.

They wake you in the morning
Before the break of day,
And send you on a circle
A hundred miles away.

All along the Yellowstone
'Tis cold the year around;
You will surely get consumption
By sleeping on the ground.

Work in Montana
Is six months in the year;
When all your bills are settled
There is nothing left for beer.

—Cowboy Song

The cowboy we see on movie and television screens usually bears little if any resemblance to the working cowboy of yesteryear. Except in the very early days, a range rider did not habitually wear a six-shooter strapped around his waist wherever he went. And when he did wear one, he did not expect to shoot at another human being. He might strap it on as a kind of ornament when he went calling on a girl of a Sunday. When he and other hands who worked for the same outfit rode into the nearest town for a Saturday night spree, he might wear it as a flaunted badge of distinction, marking him as a wild and carefree devil

This photograph, taken in 1897, shows a roundup in Ward County, Texas. The cowboys in the foreground brought in the big herd of almost 2,000 cattle seen behind them.

of the range lands. If he did, he usually had to check it at the livery stable or at the first bar, most western towns sensibly having prohibited the carrying of guns within town limits.

Of course, there were some cowboys who were belligerent by nature and who habitually carried guns that they kept cleaned and in prime condition for serious shooting. This type of cowboy often became a roaming gun fighter, attracted to places where there was range trouble. He might be hired at premium wages by ranchers' or stockgrowers' associations more as a kind of range policeman than as a cattle hand. Sometimes outlaws took temporary ranch jobs; William French, a New Mexico rancher, once had several members of the Wild Bunch, a notorious gang of bandits, working on his WS ranch for several weeks. Later, French said that Butch Cassidy, the leader of the gang, who hired out under the name Jim Lowe, was one of the best workers ever employed by the WS.

An experience told by a Badlands rancher named A. C. Huidekoper shows how much range life and love of ranch work was in the blood even of cowboys who had gone wrong. Late one afternoon, Huidekoper was finishing his day's work, branding colts in a corral, when two strangers rode up on fine saddle horses. They dismounted and perched on the corral fence to watch the work going on. Range land custom was to let them stay overnight, so the rancher told them to turn their

The famous western artist Charles Russell, many of whose paintings appear in this book, wrote and illustrated the letters that appear above and on the opposite page. The illustrations show cowboys at their usual work of roping cattle and breaking horses.

animals—the saddle horses and two pack horses—out with his night herd. The men said they wanted to make an early start in the morning and would prefer to leave the animals in the stable. When the rancher started work the next morning, he was surprised to find the men still around. When the branding got under way, they remarked that he seemed shorthanded and offered to help out. They kept at it all day; the two were crackajacks, Huidekoper said, and "worked like beavers." Again that night they left

their horses in the stable, and early the following morning they rode away. Some time later, a sheriff came to Huidekoper's place asking if the rancher had seen the two men. They had robbed a stage of $10,000 in gold, and the loot had been stowed away safely in their packs while they stayed to lend the rancher a helping hand.

The average cowboy, however, was a mounted worker for wages—a hired man on horseback. He worked hard most of the time, putting in long hours in all kinds of weather. He received from thirty to forty dollars a month, plus his keep—board and room (generally the cowboys were quartered in an outbuilding called the bunkhouse). The hands ate their meals in the ranch-

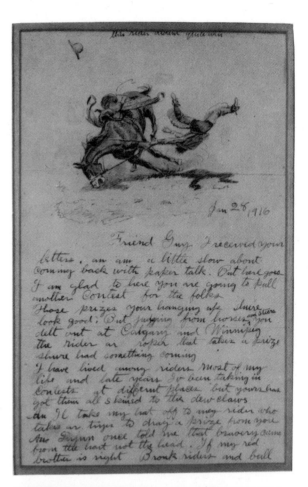

house kitchen or, often in the case of a big outfit, in a separate building. The food they were served was plentiful, if it lacked variety. Beef was the staple meat along with bacon and salt pork. Most range men were so bitterly opposed to sheep that they even refused to eat mutton when it was available, and many considered it an insult to be offered it. Bread or biscuits, coffee, potatoes, and canned tomatoes, in addition to the meat dish, made an average meal. Fresh fruit or green vegetables were almost unheard of. Dried peaches might serve for dessert. "Lick" (molasses) was a common sweetener. To keep the men happy, a good ranch cook might dish up extras such as dried fruit pies; gingerbread or ginger cake with raisins; or hot rolls with brown sugar and cinnamon on top. One cowboy favorite was "spotted pup" (rice and raisins cooked together). Almost any jelly concoction was called "shivering Liz."

The typical cowboy, who ate what he was served and generally contrived to like it however much he might grumble, was carelessly improvident, openhandedly generous, and remarkably loyal, a man who often showed reckless daring and a gay abandon that commanded respect and admiration. Living a life of wild freedom, he performed work that was onerous and often lonely in a land where danger lurked, and where courage, strength, and devotion to duty were necessary if he did properly the job he had to do. An extreme individualism, that in more settled surroundings might have been a handicap, habits of self-reliance, personal resourcefulness, and fortitude—these were hallmarks of the good cowboy.

Mack McAvoy tells the story of a Negro cowboy named George "who was not very well clad because he liked to pike at monte [gamble] too well to buy clothes. We all had coughs and colds till it was like a bunch of Texas pot hounds baying a 'possum when we tried to sleep. One bitter night I was near George on herd and tried to get him to go to the chuck wagon and turn his horse loose, but he was too game for that. His teeth were chattering as he said to me, 'I can stand it if the rest of you can.' Presently I saw him lean over his saddlehorn, coughing, and he looked like he was losing his breath. By the time I got to him, he was off his horse, as dead as a mackerel and as

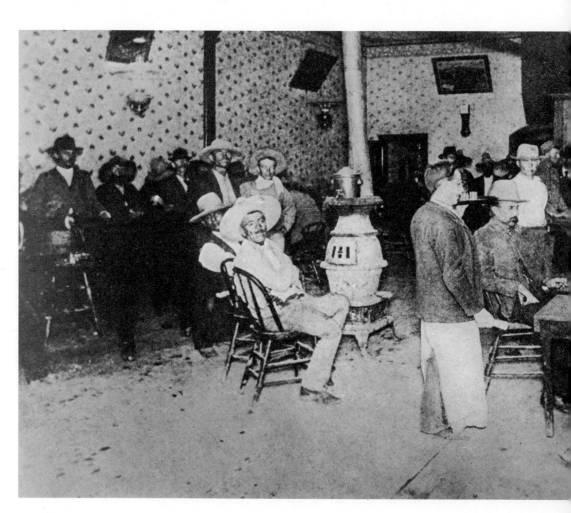

stiff as a poker. He had simply frozen to death sitting on that horse. We placed his body in the chuck wagon on his bed and drove to the Palo Duro and on the highest hill we could find we planted the poor black boy, rolled in his blankets. The ground was sandy; so we could dig a grave deep enough that the coyotes would not claw into it."

Another pervasive range land trait was honesty. When a North Dakota man called Hell Roaring Bill Jones, who was hired to dig post holes, came to collect his pay at the end of the job he refused to take any, for he had not dug one as deep as the rest. The custom of buying cattle by "range count" is another case in point: a total price was paid on the basis of the number of cattle on the range as estimated by the owner, no exact tally being attempted. Almost invariably the buyer found later that he had acquired more cattle than he had paid for. Anyone discovered in a dishonest act lost the respect of his fellows, and often found it difficult to get employment.

Naturally there were some tough customers among range men, and the great cowboy artist Charles Russell once wrote of them that they were "careless, homeless, hard-drinking men," but most observers concede that as a class they ranked high in most important respects. The loyalty that was one of their most attractive traits ran not only to their fellow workers but to the outfits they rode for. A cowboy was an "N Bar man" or a "Flying O man" or an "XIT man," and the boss could count on him to do his share, or more than his share, of all work under the most demanding or perilous circumstances. Another common cowboy trait that nearly equaled loyalty in its value to his outfit was his power of observation. His watchfulness and

Photographed in the 1880's in a saloon in Pecos, Texas, these cowboys seem to be enjoying two of their favorite pastimes, drinking and gambling. Potbellied stoves like the one seen here were the only means of heating the flimsy wooden buildings of cow towns.

In this painting by Charles Russell a group of cowboys has just arrived in a bleak Montana cow town, determined to have a good time after a period of hard work. Hands who

worked together on a ranch usually came to town together for their fun, and it was an unusual lot that behaved themselves. Russell called his picture A Wild Outfit in Town.

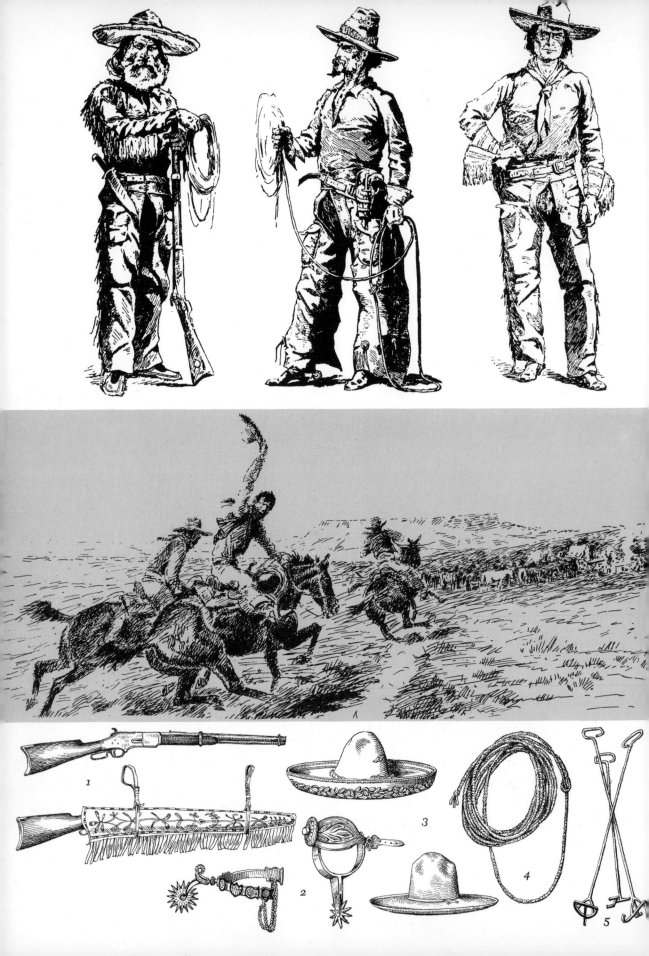

As the years passed, the cattle industry developed certain basic items of equipment that all cowboys used in their work. This did not mean, of course, that all cowboys looked alike; the American cowboy was usually a proud man who retained his individuality. The sketches above show four cowboys wearing variations of this standard equipment, and looking quite different. The sketches below show the basic gear used by most cowboys (in most cases the more elaborately decorated articles are of Mexican workmanship): (1) rifle and rifle in holder; (2) spurs; (3) broad-brimmed hats; (4) catch rope or lariat; (5) branding irons; (6) six-shooter, belt, and holster; (7) boots; (8) saddles. The picture at left shows a group of hungry cowboys, their work forgotten for the moment, racing in from the range to have their evening meal.

ability to remember small details paid off; he knew where range animals were most likely to be at different times and seasons; he knew the peculiarities of different horses and, accordingly, how they should be treated and what jobs they should be used for; he knew how stock reacted to changes in weather and in range conditions, and he was guided by that knowledge in carrying out his duties.

Eric Howard tells a tale about a range man's powers of observation: a stranger who was riding through stopped for a few minutes at a chuck wagon and then rode on; a few days later a deputy sheriff came along and asked the cook if a stranger had been around. The answer being yes, the deputy asked what the man looked like.

"Well, sir," replied the cook, "he was ridin' a dun horse with a white stockin' on its left hind foot, a loose shoe on the right, and an X-bar brand. Horse was a four-year-old. Had a mangy saddle, red and white Navaho saddle blanket, two Navaho conchas on the bridle. The man was right around five-eight, had on Levi's and a blue shirt, corduroy vest. Scar on his right cheek, runnin' down his neck inside his collar. Two–three days' beard. A sharp-eyed man, eyes kind of blue. Long nose,

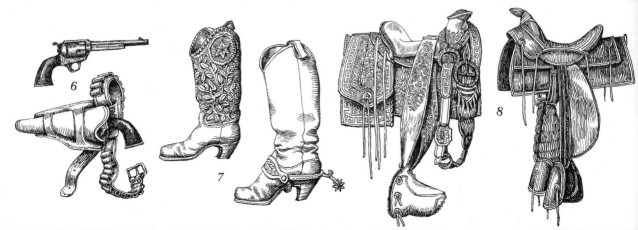

with the tip twisted to the left, like he was smellin' somethin' bad over there. Had on a J. B. Stetson hat, with a woven hair band. I didn't take a close look at him, but that's about the way he stacked up."

Wit and humor were also much in evidence among the range riders. Sometimes it was levity designed to ease him through a tight spot; sometimes it was fun for its own sake. It might be elaborate, planned joshing, or it might be an on-the-spot reaction to a situation.

Much cowboy humor was of the rough-and-ready, practical-joke kind—such as loosening saddle cinches so a rider would take a fall from his horse. The victim of such tricks was expected to react manfully, lest he be put to further and even rougher tests. If he took it in good spirit, bided his time, and retaliated successfully, he was regarded as a good fellow. Initiating newcomers to the range was a popular pastime.

The cheerful exchange of insults was a normal part of cow-country living. Once when a cowboy was eating supper at a roundup wagon, he started complaining loudly about the grub. The cook, who was not disposed to take criticism lying down, asked sarcastically, "Think you can manage to eat the biscuits, or shall I throw 'em out and try makin' up a new batch?"

"They ain't so bad," he said. "If you put a lot o' this butter on 'em you can't taste 'em quite so much. Course you kin taste the butter, but then I'm pretty

strong myself, and anyhow your coffee's weak enough to bring up the general average."

Charging a range cook with making weak coffee was well calculated to offend, as ranch people preferred theirs very strong; the classic definition of cowboy coffee had it "hot as hell, black as sin, and strong as death."

Range cooks were supposed to be sour and autocratic by nature, and many of them did their best to live up to the tradition. One who worked for a big outfit in the Black Hills laid down the law amusingly, though, displaying a large sign in the kitchen of the headquarters ranch:

IF YOU CAN'T WASH DISHES DON'T EAT.
WE USE WOOD IN THE COOKSTOVE CUT
16 INCHES LONG
BUT NO LONGER.
A BUSY COOK LOVES A FULL WOOD BOX.
A FULL WATER BUCKET MAKES
A HAPPY COOK.
STRAY MEN ARE NOT EXEMPT FROM HELPING
WASH DISHES, BRINGING WOOD OR WATER.
THE WELL IS JUST 110 STEPS FROM
THE KITCHEN,
MOSTLY DOWNHILL BOTH WAYS

Actually, many range cooks were goodhearted men, in spite of their crankiness, ready to hand out a snack to any rider who might stop at the wagon for a few minutes' break during roundup, or to give the wrangler a hand with the rope corral at noon. On roundup or on a drive, he drove the chuck wagon besides doing the cooking; and he was often expected to fill in as barber, dentist, doctor, or veterinary. If there was a fatal accident he might even be drafted to act as undertaker, since he was the custodian of the shovel, which he used for digging his fire trench. He cooked the crew's grub over an open fire, built in the dug trench, using Dutch ovens, large kettles, and a huge coffeepot. Bread dough he mixed in a dishpan. Dishes were washed in an extra-large pot called the camp kettle. The cowboys called him "coosie," tolerated his foibles, tried to keep on his good side, and when he was in a bad mood kept out of his way. According to an old range saying, "Only a fool argues with a skunk, a mule, or a cook."

Most cowboys had little if any formal education, but there were not many illiterates on the range lands. Paperbound books were offered as coupon-premiums by some tobacco manufacturers, and many cowboys

What began as a friendly game of cards between the two cowboys at center is just about to become a gun battle. The man standing at right had evidently accused the other of cheating in the game and has drawn on him.

who bought the "makin's" with which they rolled their own cigarets sent away for such books, thus augmenting local reading-matter supplies that were generally rather scanty. Some men became staunch readers who could quote Shakespeare and the Bible with equal proficiency, and a few became remarkably well-informed men. A young New Mexico cowboy named Gene Rhodes always carried books in his saddlebags and enjoyed reading them as he rode along on his horse, a practice his neighbors never forgot. In later years, he became a successful novelist and short-story writer— Eugene Manlove Rhodes, author of some of the finest books ever written about the cattle country.

Such were the men who did the day-to-day work of the cattle ranges. Most were good-natured and friendly; a minority were withdrawn or hostile. Most were fun-loving and sociable; a few were lone wolves or chip-on-the-shoulder fellows. Whatever their outlook on life or their attitude toward others, they took pride in doing their share of work and in their ability to do the job; they got things done with a minimum of supervision, each having developed early in the game an expertness and a self-sufficiency that were suited to the nature of the job and the land in which it was done.

The zest and the gaiety with which most of them carried it off were infectious and ingratiating. The average cowboy may not have been a hero, but the picture that comes down to us shows a warmly human and attractive figure.

A cowboy spent most of his time in the saddle, but not many of them cared for the strenuous and dangerous job of catching and breaking horses. The horse at right is a wild mustang who has just been roped. His strong teeth and sturdy hoofs could be deadly if the cowboy was not cautious. The rider at left is doing his best to stay in the saddle while breaking a horse.

Home
on the Range

The bronze below—called Coming Thru the Rye—*shows four cowboys celebrating by firing six-shooters into the air. Executed by the well-known western artist Frederic Remington, this piece of sculpture is one of the most famous of his studies in bronze of the American cowboy. Remington was extremely good at capturing the lines of the muscular western horses in motion.*

In the earliest years of the open-range era, a rancher generally had the exclusive use of all the range he wanted; his cattle ran by themselves, and he did not have to worry about their getting mixed in with other ranchers' stock. Later, when most of the neighboring ranges bordered on each other, rather than being separated by unused grassland, cattle with different brands inevitably got mixed together. Neighboring ranchmen began to co-operate on an informal basis, agreeing to work each other's cattle, and twice a year, in spring and fall roundup, help each to gather his own animals into one herd. This informal co-operative roundup was gradually formalized into what was called the district roundup system.

In the spring roundup, cattle that had drifted away during the winter were hunted and found and driven back to their own ranges, where calves were branded and earmarked. In the fall roundup, those animals that were to be sold for beef were herded together for shipment; stock that riders had missed in the spring or that had wandered away in the meantime were gathered; and calves born after the earlier roundup were branded. Spring roundup got under way when grass showed green, and might keep the riders working for as much as forty days. The fall gather, started about the beginning of September, generally lasted about a month.

Under the district roundup system, the associated cattlemen in a large region met in the early spring, adopted a plan for use in each district, named a roundup foreman for the district, and set a date for work to begin. The "super," or foreman, who was placed in full charge of all roundup work in his district for that year, was paid a salary by the association. Two or three days before the day set for the beginning of work, each big outfit in the district sent several men and a chuck wagon to the central meeting place; small ranchers sent one or two men each; and from ranches across the line in adjoining districts came "reps"—riders representing the interests of those ranches. In a large district, fifteen or twenty wagons and three or four hundred men might arrive by the close of the first day. The bosses of the various outfits got together with the district boss to work out detailed plans for operations and to assign duties among outfits; and the assembled cowboys spent their time renewing acquaintances, singing, playing poker, telling stories, staging wrestling matches and rodeo contests. This went on for two or three days, or until all the men had gathered and work could get started.

Before daylight a "turnout" order was given. Beds were rolled and tied; the cowboys ate a quick breakfast and roped and saddled their mounts; the cooks washed and packed the dishes; bedrolls were thrown into bed wagons (carrying bedrolls, slickers and extra coats, corral ropes, stake ropes, and other gear), and mules were hitched to

chuck wagons and the bed wagons. The riders dispersed, each heading for a small area that he was to comb for stock, after which he would drive all he found to the designated roundup ground—this was called riding circle. By noon, seven or eight thousand cattle might be gathered in one herd, milling and lowing, cows and their calves separated and bawling while

they hunted for each other. The cowboys turned their horses into the *remuda,* caught fresh ones for the afternoon's work, got something to eat—by this time the cooks had arrived with their wagons, set up camp, and prepared some food—and rode back to the herd.

Each cowboy had a string of six or more horses for his use during the

The cowboys below were photographed in 1908 as they lined up at a bar in Tascosa, Texas, to quench their thirst. They are following the old cowboy custom of not taking off their hats inside. The cowboy was almost as fond of his hat as he was of his horse.

roundup. Cutting horses—agile, quick-to-respond mounts—were used for the task of separating individual animals from the herd, either to be branded or to be thrown into a different herd. Night horses, used for herding the cattle at night, had to be quiet-tempered and sure-footed. Circle horses—used to gather the herd on the circle drive—preferably were animals with plenty of "bottom" (stamina). As a rule, only geldings were used for roundup or ordinary range work; mares tended to be nervous and skittish, stallions mean and quarrelsome.

While their circle horses rested, the cowboys mounted their cutting horses, rode into the herd, and "cut" from it those animals bearing the brands they wanted. In this task, the trained cutting horse bore the main burden, turning and twisting, forcing the cow that was wanted away from the herd and into the open, where other riders took

over and held her some distance away —the nucleus of a smaller herd, all of which would bear one brand.

While the man on the cutting horse headed back to the herd to repeat the operation, the calf—if there was one with the cow cut from the herd—was roped, dragged to the branding fire, thrown on its side and held by two men, while a third applied the red-hot branding iron to its flank quickly and carefully, so the brand was burned

This charming painting shows a camp established for a roundup at the edge of a Montana town. The hands sleep in tents, and the wagons carry supplies. This was probably a roundup of young horses rather than cattle.

neither too shallow nor too deep. While the calf was still bawling, a sharp knife was used to cut off parts of its ears. This earmarking provided a way by which riders could easily identify stock on the range. Cutting

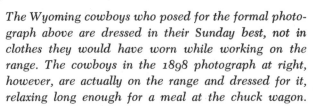

The Wyoming cowboys who posed for the formal photograph above are dressed in their Sunday best, not in clothes they would have worn while working on the range. The cowboys in the 1898 photograph at right, however, are actually on the range and dressed for it, relaxing long enough for a meal at the chuck wagon.

off the end of the ear made it "cropped"; a piece cut from the bottom was an "underbit"; from the top, "overbit." The end of the ear might be split, or shaped in some distinctive way. Except for calves, stock found on the range without earmarks were called "slick-ears" (a "slick-ear" was also a maverick, the name given to any unbranded yearling). All mavericks gathered in a general roundup were declared the property of the outfit on whose range they were found. Besides being branded and earmarked, bull calves were castrated, except a few that were judged to be prime specimens and kept as breeding stock.

Cows and calves bearing the same brand, and off their home range, were kept together in a small herd called a "cut." Animals carrying the brand of any ranch outside the district were run in with a "stray herd" until that outfit's rep rider judged he had enough

to drive back to his own range. Other brand herds were driven along until their own ranges were reached, or until the roundup work was completed. Herds were kept apart, at safe distances, day and night, by men detailed to guard them, while the other riders continued working the range, on circle, cutting out and branding the cattle.

After supper each night, the cowboys with each herd slept in beds made up on the ground, with their night horses staked out close by. One pair of men rode on the first shift of the night guard watching each herd. In a couple of hours one of them rode in from the herd to awaken the next pair due to stand watch while the other one stayed with the cattle, and so on—until, about three A.M., the cook shouted, "Roll out!" and another day began. Sometimes there were night drives, and the men rode for miles to reach a camp from which they could begin driving cattle early in the morning toward the new roundup ground. A night drive was enough to make any cowboy complain that on this job a man didn't need a bed, "all he needed was a lantern to catch a fresh horse." During the day, the *remuda* was herded by one wrangler; at night another one, called the nighthawk, took over that chore.

The super and his men faced their greatest task on the last day of work in a district. Besides the last roundup herd — or day herd — being held, cut, and branded, there were being held, close by, perhaps a dozen other herds that had been gathered previously in the district. Some of them might have been herded and driven together for several days. Some of the riders who had started out with the roundup outfit had finished their work and had gone, so that when the super had the greatest number of cattle to be handled he had the fewest men. But somehow they always managed. A good super was a diplomat who knew how to handle men, keep them working smoothly, and prevent little troubles from growing into big ones. Those who had to direct roundups in which there were crews of men from ranches unfriendly to each other often had to be mediators or judges in addition to supervising the roundup operation.

After the last day herd had been cut, the brand herds were lined out toward their own ranges. In a properly conducted roundup, nearly every ani-

mal that had drifted off its own range during winter and spring was returned to it for summer and fall. The fall roundup, in such cases, involved principally the gathering of beef cattle to be sold on the market and the branding of late calves. It was run in much the same way as the spring roundup, except that the stock to be sold were thrown into "beef herds" and at the end of the roundup were trail-driven to market, or to a railroad shipping point where they could be loaded into cattle cars.

In some regions in summer, herds were driven to higher range or mountain pastures, especially when lowland heat and summer drought began to lower the water supply. Water for stock was a problem, especially in the

southwestern range lands, and ranch hands were often occupied in moving the cattle from one locality to another, according to the changing conditions of streams and water holes. Windmills used for pumping water had to be kept in operation, and where "tanks" (earth-banked reservoirs) were used for water storage the hands had to watch the outlets carefully. Any motherless calves found on the range had to be taken to camp or headquarters ranch where they could be looked after. Doctoring for screwworms was another summer chore. Blow flies often laid their eggs in a brand wound; these hatched into maggots (screwworms) and if left alone might eat their way into a vital spot and kill the animal. When a cowboy riding range saw a calf licking at its brand he knew it had maggots; the calf was roped and thrown, the worms cleaned out of the wound, and it was daubed with a special ointment, then covered with dirt to make sure the ointment stayed on. Also during the summer, bulls were herded to different parts of the range where they were needed.

After the fall roundup, ranch work slacked off. A few of the older hands —the regulars—were kept on the pay-

In his painting of a spring roundup held in Montana in 1913 (left), Charles Russell has included several of the operations performed by a cowboy. The rider in the foreground is getting ready to rope a steer while the men working with him attempt to keep the herd from straying. At the upper right, a group of hands is busy branding recently-born calves.

129

roll. They manned the line camps (cabins located near the limits of the outfit's range, where men were usually stationed in pairs) to turn back stock that might otherwise drift away before storms; they rode the range to watch the stock and sometimes drive weak animals in for shelter or special feeding; they saw that streams and water holes were kept open. The hands who were paid off after the beef was shipped sometimes landed odd jobs in town, or spent the winter trapping animals for pelts or "wolfing" (bounty money was paid when wolves' ears were turned in); some rode the "chuck line" — going from one ranch to another, staying a couple of days, then drifting on.

Early spring work included riding bog—finding animals that were bogged in mud and getting them free of it; helping winter-weakened stock; and in general getting a line on the location and condition of the range cattle, in anticipation of the spring roundup. Preparations for the roundup were started; horses were driven in and their hoofs trimmed and horseshoes nailed on; broncos were broken to saddle — generally by professional bronc busters, or "snappers," who were paid so much per animal. Bronc snapping was a special skill and a fairly dangerous trade; and in spite of the saying, "There was never a horse that couldn't be rode, and never a man that couldn't be throwed," the average cowboy made no claim to being a horse breaker.

Chuck wagons were overhauled, their axles were greased, and later they were stocked with supplies. A chuck wagon was a light ranch wagon with a cupboard set into the tail end of the box. The forward part of the wagon bed provided space to carry potatoes, beans, bacon, carefully wrapped beef carcasses, dried fruits, coffee, "airtights" (canned goods), and other edibles. It also held some cooking utensils and other essential equipment, including branding irons. Slung underneath the wagon box, between the wheels, was a cowhide, called a "cooney," which carried other camp equipment and firewood.

The main item in each ranch hand's own equipment was his bedroll. This included a bed tarp—an oblong piece of tarpaulin; "soogans"—square-shaped quilts; and a double blanket sheet. In use, the sides of the tarp were folded up over the edges of the soogans, and half its length was brought up over the bed, or, if needed, clear over the head of the sleeping man. A cowboy kept his clean socks and shirt in a sack he called his "warbag"; carried inside the bedroll, his warbag also might contain a slicker, a number of small personal possessions, his shaving equipment, and sometimes his six-shooter, a book, or a mouth organ.

A cowboy also owned the tools of his trade: a saddle and saddle blanket; a bridle; a lariat or "catch rope," which was either a manila rope or a braided-rawhide *reata* (see glossary on page

21); a picket or stake rope; hobbles; and sometimes a quirt.

There were two principal types of cowboy saddles, identified by the regions where they first were used. The Texas saddle, used widely in the Southwest, was a "double-rigged" saddle, meaning that it was equipped with two cinches (a cinch being the saddle girth or bellyband that holds the saddle on the horse's back)—and old-time range lingo labeled it a "rimfire" rig. The California, or California-Oregon saddle, used extensively on the West Coast and in the Northwest generally, was single-rigged—having one cinch. When a single cinch was placed in the middle of the saddle, range men called it a "centerfire"; set farther forward, it became a three-quarter rig; and seven-eighths and five-eighths rigs were also developed, to suit individual needs and desires.

In the use of the lariat, or "catch rope," that indispensable tool for the working of stock, the American cowboy never quite equaled the amazing skill of most Mexican vaqueros. The experienced vaquero used more kinds of casts and developed more intricate variations than did the cowboy, whose roping repertory was generally limited to six types of rope catches. The most common one was the overhead swing,

Below, a herd crosses Powder River, which flows through Wyoming and Montana. When driving cattle across water, cowboys had to be alert for signs of panic in the herd.

All of the hands of a ranch in Wyoming posed for the photograph above in 1885. An out-fit, or staff, of this size indicates that the ranch had a fairly large herd. The wooden ranch house below, located somewhere in the Dakotas, was photographed in 1888 while the hands sat around outside. This kind of ranch house was typical of the northern cattle region. In the warmer parts of Texas, houses were often built of Mexican-style adobe brick.

used by a mounted man roping stock in the open. The hooleyann loop was used when roping from the ground, to catch saddle horses in a corral, and also in roping calves around the neck from horseback. Two other casts used principally by a roper on foot were the pitch catch, with the loop traveling in a horizontal plane; and the slip catch, with a vertical loop; in both of these, the loop was thrown direct from the starting position, not rotated above the thrower's head first. The slip catch was the best method of roping a horse by the forefeet. The heeling catch, performed from horseback, was used to rope stock by the hind feet to throw and hold them—in bringing calves to the branding fire, or to down an animal already roped by the head but not thrown; the loop was rotated in a vertical circle and slipped under the mov-

ing animal to catch the hind feet. The forefooting catch, also made from horseback, was started with the loop horizontal and above the roper's head, and executed by turning it over the running animal's shoulders while the roper rode alongside, the loop turning half over and catching both forelegs.

The length of the rope used and the method of fastening it to the saddle horn varied in different regions. Shorter ropes were used in Texas and generally throughout the Southwest, where it was the practice to tie the end of the rope to the saddle horn. Cowboys who used this method were referred to as "tie-fast" men. In California and Oregon, longer ropes were used—rawhide *reatas* were normally from fifty to sixty feet long—where the end of the rope was dallied around the saddle horn. Those using this method

U. S. Indian Brand

Lazy S

BQ
Barbecue

Too Hot
2HOT

Spanish Bit

HC
First Texas Brand
(Chisholm Ranch)

José Sepulveda Ranch

John Chisum's Long Rail

Halff's Quién Sabe
(Don't Know)

Flying X

Running W
(King Ranch)

Rocking Chair

Terrapin

Quarter Circle H

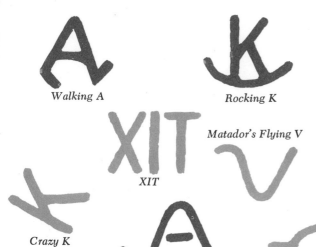

Cattle were first branded in the New World by the Spanish explorer Hernando Cortés, who had his herd marked with Christian crosses. As ranching spread in California and Texas, branding became more important. Neighboring ranchers whose herds grazed in the same area had no reason to fight over the possession of stray cattle if each animal was clearly marked. Branding also discouraged cattle rustlers—for it was hard to sell cattle marked with someone else's brand. The picture at left is a typical branding scene. Two men hold the calf down as a third man presses a heated iron into the calf's hide. As brands became more common, it began to require more imagination to invent a new or unique brand. Some of the brands shown above and below were intended to be humorous (such as the "Barbecue" and "Too Hot" brands); some indicate the owner's initials (the "First Texas Brand" and the "JA" brand); and others were chosen primarily because the designs were pleasing (such as the "Texas Mission Brand" and the "Spanish Bit"). The "H.C." of 1832 is the first known brand recorded in Texas.

Walking A

Rocking K

Matador's Flying V

XIT

Crazy K

Goodnight and Adair's JA

Hog Eye

were, naturally, "dally men." The dally method, by allowing some "give" when the roped and running steer hit the end of the line eased the strain on it, was less likely to result in a snapped rope. This was particularly important with a rawhide *reata*. Dallying was also easier both on the roped stock and on the saddle horse. Tying fast made sure that the roped animal would be held (unless the line broke), but in case of an emergency the dallied rope could be turned loose quickly, while a tied rope had to be cut. Both methods had their defenders and champions; and tying fast was reckoned a necessity for working cattle in brush country, where a rider often needed one free hand to protect his face from whipping branches. It was in such country, too, that the longer rope used in other regions would have been more bothersome than useful.

Such, then, were the seasons, the tasks, and the tools of the men who rode the cattle ranges. The tasks varied with the seasons; the tools were the constants. The tasks were confronted and accomplished, the seasons endured, the tools prized; they made up the workaday aspects of the life that most range men lived to the hilt and savored in all its hard vitality. The bone-wearying work, the long hours, were taken in stride. There was one cowboy who, when asked by a wondering observer from the East when he ever found time to sleep, only answered mildly, "Why, in the winter, same as you."

The
Spell
of
the
West

This colorful poster announced the arrival of one of Buffalo Bill's Wild West shows in an American city. The cowboy and the frontiersman of the West had become legends in their own time, and the Wild West show brought riding and shooting exhibitions, mock cowboy and Indian fights, and roping demonstrations to thrilled and fascinated audiences in the United States and Europe.

We celebrate the Old West mainly in legends. Even while it was still alive a celebrated frontiersman with a flair for showmanship — William "Buffalo Bill" Cody — organized the first great Wild West show. It offered wide-eyed audiences "Colonel" Cody, with his long hair and handsome mustache, riding his magnificent white horse and

136

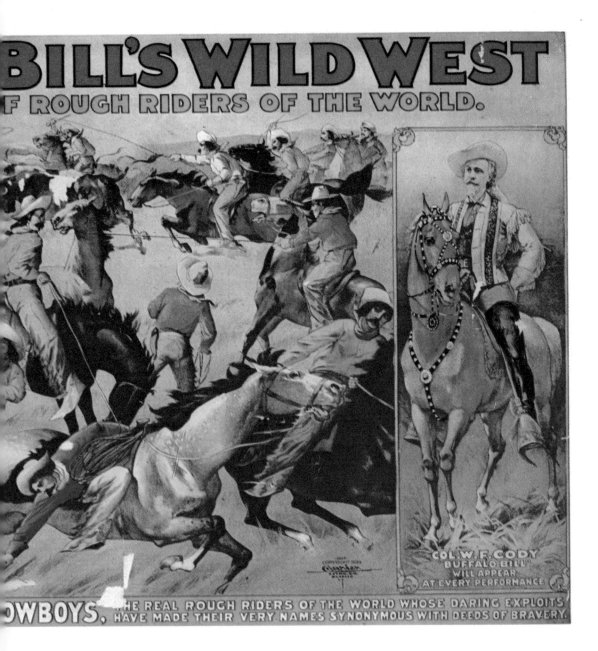

BILL'S WILD WEST
F ROUGH RIDERS OF THE WORLD.

COL. W. F. CODY
"BUFFALO BILL"
WILL APPEAR
AT EVERY PERFORMANCE

OWBOYS, THE REAL ROUGH RIDERS OF THE WORLD WHOSE DARING EXPLOITS HAVE MADE THEIR VERY NAMES SYNONYMOUS WITH DEEDS OF BRAVERY.

shooting glass balls while doing so, plus more fancy shooting by that unequaled markswoman Annie Oakley (later immortalized by the Broadway musical *Annie Get Your Gun*), and such thrilling bits as an attack on a stagecoach by a band of whooping, yipping Indians. They were honest-to-goodness red men, too; Cody even had that wily old strategist, Chief Sitting Bull of the Hunkpapa Sioux, on his show's payroll.

After several triumphal tours, including one to Europe during which England's Queen Victoria watched and approved it, Buffalo Bill's Wild West show had to face imitators and competitors. At the same time, an allied type of exhibition, with such cowboy contests as riding, roping, and steer wrestling, was developing. Called rodeo (from the Spanish-Mexican *rodeo*, meaning a going round, or roundup), it was at first a purely local entertainment event, held in connection with western fairs or Fourth of July celebrations, but it grew swiftly in popularity and attracted nationwide attention. Colonel Zack Mulhall, who ran the Mulhall Ranch in Oklahoma, included many rodeo-contest features in his famous Wild West show, which toured all over the country successfully. Lucille Mulhall, Colonel Zack's daughter, was a superb roper and a star of the show; two others in the show's great cast were Will Rogers and Tom Mix.

The Wild West shows failed to survive the depression of the 1930's and are no more, but the rodeo, descendant of the old mission roundup, and child of the cow-town celebration, has become a national institution. Professional contestants follow the circuit, appearing in as many different rodeos as they can make. The one held annually in New York's Madison Square Garden may be the epitome of rodeo professionalism, but in spite of, or perhaps because of, its slickness it seems

somehow less authentic than the ones staged in the West—Cheyenne's Frontier Days, the Calgary Stampede, and those put on in Pendleton, Prescott, Fort Worth, and scores of other places.

The movies, first for the silent screen, then the talking one, have made almost countless film dramas about the Old West, with the central character a cowboy in a majority of them. In the "silents," first William Farnum and William S. Hart, later Tom Mix, Hoot Gibson, and Harry

A modern photograph shows the opening of a rodeo in Pendleton, Oregon, one of the most important towns on the present-day rodeo circuit. The exciting events that go on inside the ring were once considered as routine activities by cowboys who worked on the range.

138

Carey, gained fame in the role of the range rider whose horsemanship, courage, and six-gun skill made him the victor over the forces of evil. Since the advent of the talking pictures, Gary Cooper and John Wayne have portrayed the cowboy-hero frequently and successfully, but Hollywood's Western films generally have failed to picture the West that was with any degree of accuracy. By and large, the horses and the scenery have been their best features.

The popularity of Western shows on television bears witness to the great interest that Americans have in their frontier past. Unfortunately, most of these TV shows have been guiltier even than the movies of presenting an inaccurate picture of the Old West. Many of these programs have been built around characters based on such real-life figures as Wyatt Earp, Wild Bill Hickok, and Bat Masterson, all of whom, besides having been trail-town peace officers, were also professional

The herd of Black Angus cattle above, photographed recently in a small Texas cow town, is being driven down the main street just as it would have been a century ago. The town itself has

changed very little since the nineteenth century. The cattle, however, are high grade beef cattle, bred from stock imported into the United States much more recently than the rangy longhorn.

gamblers and close to the frontier underworld, if not part of it. Even Johnny Ringo, who was a notorious Arizona outlaw and a drunkard who eventually committed suicide, has been presented as a champion of the law and an upholder of justice. Another show has Billy the Kid *a friend* of Sheriff Pat Garrett! A happier choice was made in the case of John Slaughter, the former Texas Ranger and Arizona rancher who was elected sheriff of Cochise County and in two terms of office cleaned the criminal element out of that region—a job that Wyatt Earp and his brothers claimed to have done earlier.

In general, literature has done better by the old-time cowboy than have the movies and television. Little can be said, it is true, for the lurid dime novels that related the purely fictional exploits of imaginary cowboys or the equally fictional adventures of such real persons as Buffalo Bill Cody or Wild Bill Hickok. Not long after the free-range era ended, Emerson Hough, who later became famous as the author of *The Covered Wagon,* wrote a novel called *The Girl at the Halfway House,* which told the story of a cattle town on the frontier. A few years later, Owen Wister's *The Virginian* was published, the first cowboy novel to become nationally known. After that there were hundreds, including many by Zane Grey and others, that were often crudely written and gave a romanticized, distorted picture of the cattle country but did succeed in transmitting some of its strength and vitality. Once in a while there has ap-

William S. Hart (center) and friends

Tom Mix

peared a novel about cowboys that has real worth and literary merit, such as *The Log of a Cowboy*, by Andy Adams, and *These Thousand Hills*, by A. B. Guthrie, Jr.; and Eugene Manlove Rhodes' short stories and novels about cattle-country people had substance besides a witty, intelligent style.

It has been in the form of the folk tale, the tall story, and the song that the spirit of the Old West has been most truly reflected. The attitude of frontier people—the zest for life, the daring, the readiness to laugh at hardship and at each other—is implicit in the verbal "stretcher," the exaggeration, as perceived by Mark Twain and recorded again and again in his book *Roughing It*. Twain was writing about mining country, not cattle kingdom, but frontier was frontier, whether the economic end product was precious metal or beef on the hoof.

It was from cowboy bunkhouse and campfire that the full-size folk tale hero came — Pecos Bill, the "great-granddaddy of all cowboys."

Pecos Bill, who was born in Texas—naturally!—was still an infant, though a mighty vigorous one, when his family decided to move farther west. One day he happened to fall out of the wagon while it was rolling along, and since he had seventeen brothers and sisters his pa and ma didn't miss him for days; by the time they did it was too late to go back and hunt for him. Little Pecos Bill was lucky, though: some coyotes found him and raised him along with their pups. He grew fast, at first running around on all fours like his foster brothers and sis-

Will Rogers   *Richard Boone*

Americans have admired cowboy heroes from the early days of silent movies to present-day television. William S. Hart was a favorite cowboy hero of the silent screen; he is shown here in a film called The Gunfighters. *Tom Mix was also a cowboy star in silent films. Will Rogers, a westerner by birth, was one of America's favorite humorists. He appeared on stage and in the movies, and was heard on radio. Richard Boone, a recent star, plays a gun fighter in a popular television series.*

144

ters. When he wanted something to play with, he kept centipedes and tarantulas for pets; and he toughened up more and got so mortal strong and so dangerous that rattlesnakes hid in the cactus when he came along because his bite might poison them. He loved his coyote foster kin, but he knew he was not a coyote himself. Like all youngsters in those days he wanted to be a cowboy, so he caught a mountain lion that he rode as a saddle horse and a giant rattlesnake that he used as a quirt. On a bet he saddled an Oklahoma cyclone and rode it across three states, leveling mountains and uprooting trees, thus creating the Texas Panhandle. Pecos Bill rode that cyclone to a standstill, until finally in desperation it rained out from under him.

Bill fell in love with a gal named Sluefoot Sue, who was nigh as strong as he was and mighty pretty besides, and they were engaged to be married. On the morning of their wedding day Sue decided she had to ride Pecos Bill's famous horse, Widow Maker. Sluefoot Sue was a champion horsewoman, and before that no bronc had ever thrown her, but Widow Maker gave just one buck and Sue went up so high she had to duck to miss hitting

The wildest and most colorful moments in the history of the Old West are those best remembered today. The painting at left by Charles Russell records the storming of a gambling house by a group of angry cowboys —and their horses. Events of this sort have been woven into the plots of innumerable novels, movies, radio and television shows.

the moon. She was wearing a fancy steel-spring bustle, so when she finally came down and hit the ground she bounced back up again just as high as before. That kept on happening, over and over, and after she had been bouncing for four days and four nights Bill had to shoot her so she wouldn't starve to death. It was the one great tragedy in Pecos Bill's life.

Another tall tale concerned two Texas cowpokes who had been sent out to build a fence. On the way to the job they found a den of hundreds of giant rattlesnakes that had been frozen stiff by a norther. They put their ropes around a bundle of these snakes, which were as straight and hard as running irons, and dragged them to where the fence had to be built. While one man held a stiffened-out snake with its tail pointed to the ground, the other would pound it in. They finished that fencing job in a hurry, and the boss was tickled pink by all the saving in time and labor, not to mention in the cost of materials. But when he rode out to see the fence, those two cowhands had to roll their blankets and mosey on—the sun had come out so hot and fierce it thawed out those cussed snakes and they had wriggled away, carrying off two miles of brand-new barbed wire.

Some of the old-time cowmen told wondrous stories about the things that happened on range and trail, often boasting of the wisdom and prowess of their cattle. In Dobie's *The Longhorns,* Shanghai Pierce told about the time he drove a thousand big Texas steers up to New Orleans. The mud and water of those Louisiana swamps had them all picking their way carefully. "My steers were nice, fat, slick critters that knew how to swim but they were used to a carpet of prairie grass. They were mighty choosy as to where they put their feet. They had a bushel of sense, and purty soon they got to balancing theirselves on logs and roots in order to keep out of that slimy mud. Yes, they got so expert that one of them would walk a cypress knee up to the stump, jump over it, land on a root and walk it out for another jump. If there was a bad bog hole between cypresses, you'd see a steer hang his horns in a mustang grapevine or maybe a wisteria and swing across like a monkey. The way they balanced and jumped and swung made my horse laugh."

The weather has always played a vital part in the lives and fortunes of people in the cattle country. The protracted droughts of recent years produced many stories like the one about the ten-year-old frog that drowned in a rainstorm because he had never learned how to swim. Many years ago, Montana's rugged weather furnished the basis for many a good yarn. Some trail drivers from Texas asked an old Montana bullwhacker about the territory's climate. "I'll tell you what kind of a climate it is," he said. "You want a buffalo coat, a linen duster, and a slicker with you all the time."

Vivid as these tall tales and legends are, it is in the rambling, plaintive, lonely verses of a cowboy song that the feeling of the Old West often comes through best. Who can hear one of these slow cattle lullabies, these almost Spanish laments, without seeing the plains at night, sensing the space, hearing the heavy movement of resting but wary cattle? The cowboy sang to his herd; he sang at the campfire, in the bunkhouse, and when he was lonesome. His song is our inheritance.

All over the West, when the cowboy reached for his guitar he told his stories in songs like this—rolling the time to the beat of a walking horse.

I made up my mind to change my way
And quit my crowd that was so gay,
And leave the girl who promised me her hand
And head down south to the Rio Grande.

'Twas in the spring of '53
When A. J. Stinson hired me,
He said, "Young feller, I want you to go
And drive this herd down to Mexico."

O, it was a long and toilsome go
As we rode on to Mexico,
With laughter light and cowboy song
To Mexico as we rolled along.

When I returned to my native land
My girl had married a richer man,
They said she'd married a richer life
Therefore wild cowboy, seek another wife.

Oh it's curse your gold and your silver too
Confound the girl who won't prove true
I'll head out west where the bullets fly
And stay on the trail till the day I die.

When the barbed-wire fence came,

The western ballads remembered today were handed down by men such as the old cowboy in this painting.

the open range began to go. So did the longhorns, giving way to other breeds of range cattle, less impressive to some eyes, with shorter horns and shorter legs—but packing more meat. And, as some grizzled cattleman is supposed to have said, "Fat's the purtiest color there is!"

No more would the range lands see such larger-than-life characters as John Chisum, the "king of the Pecos," who in spring roundup each year branded twenty thousand calves with a straight line running from shoulder to tail, a mark that other cowmen were quick to call the Fence Rail. Not again would there be a Charlie Goodnight to defy armed Kansans and drive his cattle across their lands, then turn around in after years and deny Richard King and Shanghai Pierce permission for their herds to pass across his range. No more would sweating, shouting riders prod northbound beef critters into the waters of Red River; nor desperate men squeeze off rifle shots through cabin windows at besieging vigilantes.

Not that big-ranch country disappeared. Quite a few of the larger outfits hung on, and have done so even to the present day, especially in the Southwest. True, the Texas Panhandle's giant XIT, which once spread over three million acres in ten counties, was broken up. But the King Ranch, with its renowned Running W brand, today has nearly one million acres in its four operating units, with approximately 100,000 cattle and 10,000 horses. New Mexico's Bell Ranch, once half-a-million acres big, has been split into four parts and sold —the one retaining the old Bell brand covers 130,000 acres. There are still about a thousand ranches in the United States that have more than 20,000 acres.

Cattle ranching today, however, with the advent of specialization, controlled breeding, business-management methods, and scientific conservation practices, has little of the glamour and adventure that marked it during the days of the cattle kingdom. Jeeps, pickup trucks, and even airplanes and helicopters have largely replaced the horse, and little of the romantic glow that surrounded the Old West saga remains. The big ranches, like the smaller ones, are now fenced in.

Something remains, though. There are still cowboys who ride horses to herd cattle, and who live in bunkhouses. Roundups are still held, with calves branded in spring and beeves gathered in fall. There are still men who would rather work on a cattle ranch than hold any other job in the world—and they are so envied that every year huge numbers of people spend their vacations in range country so they can play at being range riders; and as the calm trail horses trudge behind the safe guide along the arroyos, perhaps they can hear in the clatter of hooves on the stones, or catch in the great arid space, a glimmer of what it all was like.

This humorous drawing from an 1874 history of the cattle trade makes fun of the earnest attempt of ranchers to stamp out disease in cattle.

AMERICAN HERITAGE PUBLISHING CO., INC.

BOOK DIVISION

Editor
Richard M. Ketchum

JUNIOR LIBRARY

Editor
Ferdinand N. Monjo

Assistant Editors
Mary Lee Settle • John Ratti

Editorial Assistants
Julia B. Potts • Mary Leverty
Malabar S. Brodeur • Judy Sheftel

Copy Editor
Naomi W. Wolf

Art Director
Emma Landau

Appendix

PICTURE CREDITS

The source of each picture used in this book is listed below, by page. When two or more pictures appear on one page, they are separated by semicolons. The following abbreviations are used:

AC—Amon Carter Museum of Western Art, Fort Worth
CSD—Carl S. Dentzel Collection
IES—Irwin E. Smith Photograph; Library of Congress, Courtesy Mrs. L. M. Pettis

HSM—Historical Society of Montana
KG—Kennedy Galleries
LC—Library of Congress
NYPL—New York Public Library
PP—Panhandle-Plains Hist. Soc.
RH—Robert Honeyman Collection

TC—*The Cattleman*, Fort Worth
TG—Thomas Gilcrease Institute of American History and Art, Tulsa
UT—University of Texas, Austin
UWL—University of Wyoming Library
YUL—Yale University Library

Cover: "Cowboy Roping a Steer," Charles Russell—Woolaroc Museum, Bartlesville, Okla. **Front End Sheet:** "Vaqueros, Rounding Up a Herd of Horses," James Walker—CSD. **Half Title:** Joseph McCoy, *Historic Sketches of the Cattle Trade,* 1874—NYPL. **Title:** "Sizing Up the Herd," Walker—CSD. **Contents:** "Arizona Vaquero," W. L. Snyder—CSD. **10** Vitus Wackenreuder—RH. **11** Henri Penélon—Charles W. Bowers Memorial Museum. **12** Charles de Granville, *Les Raretés des Indes*—NYPL. **13** IES. **14-5** "Charros at the Roundup," Walker—KG. **16** (both) William Rich Hutton—Henry E. Huntington Lib. & Art Gallery. **18-9** (top) "Roping the Bear at Santa Margarita," Walker—Calif. Hist. Soc.; (bot.) William Meyer, *Journals,* 1841-43—Bancroft Lib. **21** "Corriendo El Gallo," Alexander F. Harmer—Coll. Howard G. Park. **22-3** W. G. M. Samuels—WM, Courtesy Bexar County. **25** (top) T. Gentilz—Witte Museum; (bot.) "Slaughtering the Beef at the Rancho," Walker—Coll. Mrs. Reginald Walker. **27** Independence Courthouse, Mo. **28-9** "Blue Bonnets," Porfirio Salinas—C. R. Smith Coll. **30-1** McCoy, *op. cit.*—NYPL. **32-3** Anon.—RH. **34** YUL. **35** (top l. to r.) PP; PP; Okla. Hist. Soc.; (bot.) TC. **36-7** Carl G. Von Iwonski—WM, Muensenberger Coll. **39** McCoy, *op. cit.*—NYPL. **40** "No Chance To Arbitrate," Russell—AC. **42-3** "A Dash for Timber," Frederic Remington—AC. **44** (top) Sedalia, Mo. Pub. Lib.; (mid. & bot.) Kansas Hist. Soc. **46-7** Louis Hoppe—WM. **48-9** IES. **50-1** (both) Frank Reaugh—UT. **53** "On Day Herd," Russell—HSM, Courtesy Frederick G. Renner. **55** IES. **56-7** "Laugh Kills Lonesome," Russell—HSM, Courtesy TC. **58-9** James Cox, *Hist. & Biog. Record of the Cattle Industry*—Denver Pub. Lib. **60-1** "Toll Collectors," Russell—HSM. **62** Princeton University Lib. **64-5** "Stampede," Remington—TG, Courtesy TC. **66-7** YUL. **68** (both) Old Print Shop. **70-1** "Caught in the Act," Russell—HSM. **72** UT. **75** Allan L. Rock, © 1961 Pawnee Bill Archives. **77** (top) New-York Hist. Soc.; (bot. l.) Swift & Co.; (bot. r.) KG. **78** (top) "An Argument with the Town Marshal,"

Remington—Estate of John R. Black, Dallas, Courtesy TC. **78-9** (bot.) Russell—AC. **79** (top) Russell—Hammer Galleries; (bot.) Russell—©The Leader Co. **81** (top) William Gallings—HSM, Courtesy TC; (bot.) Cassidy—John R. Black Estate, Courtesy TC. **82-3** (both) Charles J. Belden, St. Petersburg, Fla. **84-5** "The Fight for the Waterhole," Remington—Museum of Fine Arts of Houston. **86** (top, both) State Hist. Soc. N. Dak.; (bot. l.) Theodore Roosevelt Assoc.; (bot. r.) Harvard University. **88-9** "When Guns Speak, Death Settles Dispute," Russell—TG. **90** TC. **91** YUL. **92-3** T. R. Davis—CSD. **95** (top l.) Culver Service; (top r.) Museum of New Mexico; (bot.) Ken Cobean, Roswell, N. Mex. **96-7** "What an Unbranded Cow Has Cost," Remington—Newhouse Galleries. **99** (top) UWL; (mid., all) UWL; (bot.) HSM. **100** CSD. **101** "The Foothill Nester," Olaf Seltzer—HSM. **102** HSM. **103** (top) Moorhouse Coll., University of Oregon Lib.; (bot.) Nebraska State Hist. Soc. **104-5** "Breaking Camp," Russell—HSM. **106-7** UT Lib. **108-9** Russell—AC. **110-11** N. R. Rose Coll. **112-13** "A Wild Outfit in Town," Russell—CSD. **114-15** (top, all) NYPL; (mid.) "Race for the Grub Wagon," Russell—HSM; (bot.) equipment drawn expressly for this book by Douglas Gorsline. **117** "Saloon Scene," Russell—Coll. J. Michael Flinn. **118** IES. **119** Magnum. **120-21** Metropolitan Museum of Art. **122-23** IES. **124-25** "Utica Picture," Russell—AC. **126** Wyoming State Lib. **126-27** UT Lib. **128-29** "The Roundup," Russell—HSM. **131** Title Insurance & Trust Co., Los Angeles. **132** Wyoming State Lib. **132-33** LC. **134** IES. **134-35** Brands drawn expressly for this book by Cal Sachs. **136-37** LC. **138-39** Univ. of Oregon Lib. **140-41** TC. **142** (both) Museum of Modern Art. **143** (l.) Brown Bros.; (r.) Columbia Broadcasting System. **144** "In Without Knocking," Russell—AC. **147** "Home Ranch," Thomas Eakins—Philadelphia Museum of Art. **149** McCoy, *op. cit.*—NYPL. **Back End Sheet:** "Cattle Drive in the San Fernando Valley," James Walker—California Historical Society.

BIBLIOGRAPHY

Abbott, E. C., and Huntington, Helen. *We Pointed Them North*. New York: Farrar & Rinehart, 1939.

Adams, Andy. *The Log of a Cowboy*. Boston: Houghton Mifflin, 1927.

Adams, Ramon F. (ed.). *The Best of the American Cowboy*. Norman, Oklahoma: University of Oklahoma Press, 1957.

Bechdolt, Frederick R. *Tales of the Old-Timers*. New York and London: The Century Co., 1924.

Billington, Ray Allen. *The Far Western Frontier, 1830-1860*. New York: Harper & Bros., 1956.

Botkin, B. A. *A Treasury of Western Folklore*. New York: Crown Publishers, 1951.

Brisbin, James. *The Beef Bonanza: or, How to Get Rich on the Plains*. Norman: University of Oklahoma Press, 1959.

Bronson, Edgar. *Cowboy Life on the Western Plains*. New York: Grosset & Dunlap, 1910.

Brown, Mark H., and Felton, W. R. *Before Barbed Wire*. New York: Henry Holt, 1956.

Carpenter, Will Tom. *Lucky 7: A Cowman's Autobiography*. Austin, Texas: University of Texas Press, 1957.

Chapman, Charles. *History of California: The Spanish Period*. New York: Macmillan, 1921.

Cleland, Robert Glass. *The Cattle on a Thousand Hills*. San Marino, California: The Huntington Library, 1951.

Dale, Edward Everett. *Cow Country*. Norman: University of Oklahoma Press, 1942.

———. *The Range Cattle Industry*. Norman: University of Oklahoma Press, 1960.

Dobie, J. Frank. *The Longhorns*. Boston: Little, Brown & Co., 1941.

———. *On the Open Range*. Dallas: The Southwest Press, 1931.

———. *A Vaquero of the Brush Country*. Dallas: The Southwest Press, 1929.

Dodge, Richard. *The Plains of the Great West*. New York: Archer House, 1959.

Drago, Harry Sinclair. *Wild, Woolly and Wicked: The History of the Kansas Cow Towns and the Texas Cattle Trade*. New York: Clarkson N. Potter, 1960.

Forrest, Earle R. *Arizona's Dark and Bloody Ground*. Caldwell, Idaho: Caxton Printers, Ltd., 1950.

Frantz, Joe B., and Choate, Julian E. *The American Cowboy: The Myth and the Reality*. Norman: University of Oklahoma Press, 1955.

Gard, Wayne. *The Chisholm Trail*. Norman: University of Oklahoma Press, 1954.

Gregg, Josiah. *Commerce of the Prairies*, ed. Max Moorhead. Norman: University of Oklahoma Press, 1954.

Haley, J. Evetts. *The XIT Ranch of Texas*. Norman: University of Oklahoma Press, 1953.

Horgan, Paul. *Great River: The Rio Grande in North American History*. New York: Holt, Rinehart and Winston, 1954.

Hough, Emerson. *The Story of the Cowboy*. New York: D. Appleton, 1910.

Howard, Joseph K. *Montana, High, Wide and Handsome*. New Haven: Yale University Press, 1943.

Hunt, Frazier. *Cap Mossman, Last of the Great Cowmen*. New York: Hastings House, 1951.

———. *The Tragic Days of Billy the Kid*. New York: Hastings House, 1956.

Keleher, William A. *Violence in Lincoln County, 1869-1881*. Albuquerque: University of New Mexico Press, 1957.

Lang, Lincoln A. *Ranching With Roosevelt*. Philadelphia: Lippincott, 1926.

Lavender, David. *Land of Giants: The Drive to the Pacific Northwest*. Garden City, N. Y.: Doubleday, 1958.

McReynolds, Edwin C. *Oklahoma: A History of the Sooner State*. Norman: University of Oklahoma Press, 1954.

Mercer, A. S. *The Banditti of the Plains*. Norman: University of Oklahoma Press, 1959.

Mora, Jo. *Californios*. Garden City, N. Y.: Doubleday, 1949.

Neider, Charles (ed.). *The Great West*. New York: Coward-McCann, 1958.

Raine, William and Barnes, Will. *Cattle*. Garden City, N. Y.: Doubleday, Doran Co., 1930.

Sandoz, Mari. *The Cattlemen*. New York: Hastings House, 1958.

Schmitt, Martin F. (ed.). *The Cattle Drives of David Shirk*. Portland, Oregon: Champoeg Press, 1956.

Toole, K. Ross. *Montana: An Uncommon Land*. Norman: University of Oklahoma Press, 1959.

Towne, Charles and Wentworth, Edward. *Cattle and Men*. Norman: University of Oklahoma Press, 1955.

Vestal, Stanley. *Dodge City: Queen of the Cow Towns*. London: Peter Nevill Ltd., 1955.

Ward, Fay E. *The Cowboy at Work*. New York: Hastings House, 1958.

Webb, Walter Prescott. *The Great Plains*. Boston: Ginn & Co., 1931.

———. (ed.). *The Handbook of Texas*. 2 vols. Austin: Texas State Historical Association, 1952.

Wellman, Paul. *The Trampling Herd*. New York: Carrick & Evans, 1939.

Zornow, William F. *Kansas: A History of the Jayhawk State*. Norman: University of Oklahoma Press, 1957.

FOR FURTHER READING

Young readers seeking further information on cowboys and cattle country will find the following books to be both helpful and entertaining.

Bauer, Helen. *California Mission Days*. Garden City, N.Y.: Doubleday, 1951.

Dobie, J. Frank. *Up the Trail from Texas*. New York: Random House, 1955.

Emrich, Duncan. *The Cowboys Own Brand Book*. New York: Thomas Y. Crowell, 1954.

Felton, Harold W. (ed.). *Cowboy Jamboree: Western Songs and Lore*. New York: Knopf, 1951.

———. *Pecos Bill: Texas Cowpuncher*. New York: Knopf, 1949.

Garst, Shannon. *Cowboys and Cattle Trails*. Chicago: Wheeler, 1948.

———. *Buffalo Bill*. New York: Messner, 1948.

Grant, Bruce. *Cowboy Encyclopedia*. Chicago: Rand McNally, 1951.

Havighurst, Walter. *Buffalo Bill's Great Wild West Show*. New York: Random House, 1957.

———. *The Great Plains*. Grand Rapids, Michigan: Fideler, 1951.

Henry, Will. *The Texas Rangers*. New York: Random House, 1957.

Holt, Stephen. *We Were There with the California Rancheros*. New York: Grosset & Dunlap, 1959.

James, Will. *Cow Country*. New York: Charles Scribner's Sons, 1927.

Roosevelt, Theodore. *The Ranch Life and the Hunting-Trail*. New York: Century, 1915.

Rounds, Glen. *Rodeo; Bulls, Broncs and Buckaroos*. New York: Holiday House, 1949.

Shapiro, Irwin. *The Golden Book of California*. New York: Golden Press, 1961.

ACKNOWLEDGMENTS: The editors wish expressly to thank the following individuals and organizations for their co-operation and generous assistance in furnishing pictorial information and material: Mr. Richard B. Duffy, Business Manager of the Historical Society of Montana; Mrs. J. Lee Johnson III, Mrs. Katrine Deakins, and Miss Maria Naylor of the Amon Carter Museum of Western Art in Fort Worth; Mr. Henry Biederman, Editor of *The Cattleman*; Dr. Harold McCracken, Director of the Whitney Gallery of Western Art in Cody; Mr. Frederick G. Renner of Washington, D. C.; Mr. Carl S. Dentzel, Director of the Southwest Museum in Los Angeles; Mr. C. Boone McClure, Director of the Panhandle-Plains Historical Society; Mr. Patrick Patterson, Director, Woolaroc Museum, Bartlesville, Okla.; and Mr. Charles E. Fulkerson, Director of Press Relations, Title Insurance & Trust Co., Los Angeles.

NYPL

Index

Bold face indicates pages on which maps or illustrations appear